Homeowner Survival Guide - the Housing Bubble

Andrew C. Mungar

AuthorHouse™
1663 Liberty Drive
Bloomington, IN 47403
www.authorhouse.com
Phone: 1-800-839-8640

First published by AuthorHouse 8/14/2009

ISBN: 978-1-4490-1722-4 (e)
ISBN: 978-1-4490-1721-7 (sc)
ISBN: 978-1-4490-1722-4 (e)

Printed in the United States of America
Bloomington, Indiana

This book is printed on acid-free paper.

Table of Contents

Foreword

This *Homeowner Survival Guide* is dedicated to help homeowners understand and resolve all the problems associated with the devastating financial crisis and the housing bubble that started in late 2007. While there is an abundance of media coverage on these problems and an abundance of private and government programs offering help, most homeowners are confused and filled with uncertainty. Many have exhausted their savings, and are now unable to make mortgage payments. They are being pulled in all directions, like revolving doors, and often end up getting nowhere:

Door #1 -The government launched a number of programs to help troubled homeowners but very few will qualify.

Door #2 -Scam artists flooded the market to take advantage of these distressed homeowners.

Door #3 -Many consultants, offered help, are asking for thousands of dollars from homeowners who cannot afford to pay their mortgages.

Door #4 –The media is urging homeowners to visit HUD counseling centers, but they find themselves in long lines only to be redirected to other options available to them.

Door #5 -Lenders publicly announced they want to help homeowners reduce their payments, but most applications are rejected because most borrowers have no idea what to submit or how to qualify.

Homeowners are led to believe there is a simple solution waiting for them behind each of the doors. In reality, it is anything but simple. Lender is so backed up with refinance, short sale, and loan modification requests that it often takes a long time before it gets to your application. It would be devastating if you get rejected for missing the slightest bit of information, or slightly off lender's target budget figure. You will then have to start all over again, from the bottom of the stack, while your home is on the verge of being foreclosed. While everyone (other than the scam artists) shares the common goal, to stop more foreclosures and to recharge the credit market, the road to recovery has been slow and frustrating.

What the troubled homeowners need is a "first aid kit" that contains everything needed to help them stop the bleeding, and provides cure over the long run. Homeowners need a complete one-stop manual, in plain language, that contains all the options available to them, the guidelines of each option, lenders contact information, qualification requirements of each lender, and step-by-step instructions on how to prepare and submit a package that is acceptable to their lenders. Americans will then able to make an informed decision, apply for a program they will qualify, and avoid wasted time and money. They will come prepared with a completed package of documents that lenders require. The entire process will move 100 times faster and more homes would be saved from foreclosures.

This *Homeowner Survival Guide* is intended to do just that, providing one stop guidance to connect all the "Doors", assisting not only the troubled homeowner, but will also provide valuable knowledge that every homeowner should have in case they run into financial hardship. This book is based on my thirty years experience in real estate consulting, having survived through Houston's housing bubble in the 80's, plus a lot of insider information derived from extensive researches, investigations, and interviews of loss mitigation negotiators, loan modification consultants, debt settlement consultants, attorneys, fund managers, etc. It also includes my personal encounters with scam artists and as a government witness to put scam artists behind bars. Not only that this guide book can help millions of homeowners, it will also relieve a lot of pressure on the lenders' loss mitigation department, so that they can operate more efficiently and ultimately approve far more homeowners needing help. Our government is spending billions of dollars to try to help troubled homeowners. With the help of this *Homeowner Survival Guide*, it will help achieving its goals faster, and far more cost effective. There was an old Chinese saying stated, "It's better to teach someone how to fish than to give him the fish". Knowledge is powerful. Together, Americans helping each other will survive this crisis.

Andrew C. Mungar, Author

Chapter 1: What Went Wrong?

Young Bryan moved to Texas and bought a donkey from a farmer for $100. The farmer agreed to deliver the donkey the next day. The next day he drove up and said, "Sorry Son, but I have bad news. The donkey died."

Bryan replied, "Well, then just give me my money back."

The farmer said, "Can't do that. I went and spent it already."

Bryan said, "Okay then, just bring me the dead donkey."

The farmer asked, "What ya gonna do with him?"

Bryan said, "I'm going to raffle him off."

The farmer said, "You can't raffle off a dead donkey!"

Bryan said, "Sure I can. Watch me. I just won't tell anybody he's dead."

A month later, the farmer met up with Bryan and asked, "What happened with that dead donkey?"

Bryan said, "I raffled him off. I sold 500 tickets at $2 a piece and made a profit of $998, less the $100 I gave you."

The farmer said, "Didn't anyone complain?"

Bryan said, "Just the guy who won. So I gave him his $2 back".

Young Bryan grew up and became an investment banker at Lehman Brothers. Someone came up with the above joke which, in many ways, reflects what happened in the real world, which is not a laughing matter.

What Went Wrong with the Whole Financial System?

Since the creation of the Federal National Mortgage Association (Fannie Mae) in 1938, and the subsequent creations of the Government National Mortgage Association (Ginnie Mae) in 1968 and the Federal Home Loan Mortgage Corporation (Freddie Mac) in 1970 to provide funds in the secondary mortgage market, the U.S. home mortgage business has been growing steadily, without major problems. The current mortgage and financial crisis was caused by subprime mortgage loans, which started only about seven years ago.

Investors and pension funds traditionally invested their money in safe U.S. Treasury Bills. When the T-Bill yield dropped to about 1 percent, investors were searching for higher yield alternative investments. At the same time, the Fed Funds rate was so low that banks saw it as a great opportunity to borrow money from the government so they could make money off of it. Meanwhile, on the other side of the world, China, Japan and the Middle East all enjoyed booming times, and they accumulated huge surpluses. They too were looking for good investments abroad. As a result, there was a huge pile of cash available searching for good investments.

All eyes were on home values which had been rising rapidly over the years in many markets like California, Florida, and Nevada, and no end was in sight. As a result, lenders decided to expand their investments in the primary mortgage market, which appeared to be safe and to be producing relatively high yields. Consumers, on the other hand, were also convinced that buying homes was a great investment. It was a perfect match of high demand for homes and high supply of money. To compete among each other, lenders became more aggressive, and homebuyers were able to obtain mortgage loans with little or no down payment. Mortgage brokers were also enjoying a booming business by simply luring homebuyers to lenders and making huge commissions along the way. Everybody won, or so it seemed.

Finally, investment bankers wanted a part of the action. They, too, flocked into the secondary mortgage market, wanting to buy home mortgages. A mortgage is seen by investment bankers as a stream of cash flow that can be bought, sold, sliced, and securitized in the secondary market. Lenders loved the opportunity to sell more mortgages in the secondary market. Not only did they make lofty profits in fees and interest spread, it also freed up their capital which enabled them to generate more mortgage loans to more homebuyers. Most importantly, once they sold the mortgages, their risk on those loans was gone. The risk was pushed down to the next level of investors.

Mortgage-Backed Securities/Collateralized Debt Obligations

Banks typically originated retail mortgage loans and sold them to Fannie Mae and Freddie Mac almost immediately. Some banks may hold some mortgages in-house to collect payments for their cash flow. Fannie Mae and Freddie Mac, then pooled together large groups of mortgages and sold them in aggregate to Wall Street investment bankers and brokerage firms as Mortgage-Backed Securities (MBSs). The investment bankers, on the other hand, became even more creative. First they borrowed millions of dollars and bought thousands of mortgages from Fannie Mae or Freddie Mac. Then they packaged hundreds of millions of dollars of Mortgage-Backed Securities in three slices:

Slice A: The safest slice, which they insured for a small fee and obtained the highest AAA bond rating from rating agencies

Slice B: The average slice, which they insured and obtained a relatively good BBB bond rating

Slice C: The risky slice, which they did not bother to insure

They sold these packages as Collateralized Debt Obligations, or CDOs, to various types of investors for hefty profits and fees. Mortgage payments coming in from homeowners paying off their loans were pooled together. It first fulfilled the obligation of Slice A, then Slice B, and any remaining money went to Slice C. Because of the AAA bond rating, the investment banker was able to sell the Slice A to the foreign governments, insurance companies, pension funds, and banks that only wanted the safest or highest credit-rated investments. Even though the rate of return for Slice A is much lower than the other two Slices, it returned a higher yield than T-Bill rates. Next, the investment banker sold Slice B to other investors, which provided a very good rate of return, and appeared to be relatively safe. Finally, the investment banker sold Slice C to hedge funds, which are for investors willing to take a higher risk in exchange for a very high rate of return. If some homeowners in the package did not pay and defaulted on their mortgages, less money would come in, and Slice C would be the first to suffer any loss. However, since home prices kept going higher, the investors were not worried. They assumed they could recover any losses from foreclosure sales. Soon, every investment banker was doing the same thing; selling CDOs and making millions of dollars along the way. At the same time, investors from all over the world were happy because they finally found a good alternative investment.

Investors were so pleased, they wanted to buy more CDO packages. So the investment bankers called up Fannie Mae, Freddie Mac, and the lenders, wanting to buy more mortgages. The lenders, in turn, called up their mortgage brokers, wanting more qualified homebuyers. One day, the brokers told their lenders they couldn't find any more qualified buyers who did not already have a mortgage. The lenders did not want to stop something that was going so well, so they started adding more risk in order to generate more and more new mortgages. They came up with a new product: "no doc, stated income" loans with zero or low down payment, no documentation, and no income verification. So, instead of following traditionally sound lending practices to responsible homeowners, the lenders started offering mortgages to subprime borrowers. These are commonly known as the subprime mortgages, which are also referred to by many as "liar loans". I call them "misstated income loans", to soften the tone. This was a major turning point.

Mortgage brokers welcomed the "no doc" loans, which made mortgages available to families who otherwise would not have qualified for a home loan. Consumers welcomed the "no doc" loans, which helped them get into a dream home. Congress welcomed the "no doc" loans because it helped move more people into homeownership. The lenders were not worried, because the moment they sold the subprime mortgages in the secondary market, their risk was gone. The investment bankers were not worried, because the moment they sold the CDO packages to investors downstream, it became someone else's risk. No one cared whether the subprime borrowers could afford their mortgage obligations. It was like a time bomb being passed around.

Chapter 2: The Subprime Mortgage Disaster

Most people have heard of subprime mortgages and the big disaster it created, but few fully understand how it created such a devastating blow to the entire financial market? In this chapter, I will provide you with some behind-the-scenes stories that may shock you! In reality, it involved tens of millions of people committing loan fraud, some minor and some serious crimes. Let's discuss how subprime mortgages work. Typical mortgages for prime borrowers require employment verification, supported by W-2 forms, tax returns, bank statements, and many other requirements in order to be qualified for a loan. For subprime borrowers, lenders, led by Countrywide Financial Corp., accept risky "no doc, stated income" loans without proof of income or employment, at slightly higher interest rates.

No Doc, "Misstated" Income Loans

For subprime borrowers, lenders only required the following to qualify:

1. A relatively clean credit report with a credit score of approximately 680 or above (some even allowed a credit score below 680)
2. Income stated by the borrower that meets the income requirement without any verification or documentation
3. An appraisal showing the property meets the loan-to-value (LTV) ratio.

Here are some of the loopholes of these easy-to-qualify requirements:

The subprime loan's qualification relied heavily on the credit score and credit report. People with little or no credit history, such as a new college grad or an entry level employee with a couple of credit cards or an auto loan, typically have a credit score of about 700. There is also a way that you may be able to "manipulate" your credit score, which I will discuss in chapter 31. This means just about anyone without a bad credit history could qualify. People with a bankruptcy on their credit report could qualify if their score was 680 or above. A credit score provides no assurance that a borrower can afford to repay a mortgage.

Without any verification of income, lenders relied solely on the income that borrowers stated (or "misstated") on their application. As a result, most borrowers "misstated" their income, just to get the loan, assuming that they could get away with it because there was no verification.

The shocking news is that, many mortgage brokers (and even some loan officers at major banks) frequently encouraged their borrowers to lie about their income. Here is how they did it: Assume a mortgage lender or broker is dealing with an entry level worker making $50,000 a year, wanting to buy a $200,000 home. He has enough savings to make a 5 percent down payment and has a decent credit score of 700. To qualify for a $190,000 loan at 7 percent, 30 year fixed mortgage, the borrower will need an annual income of about $79,000. During the application process, the mortgage broker or the lender will tell the applicant verbally (it's always verbal so they will not get in trouble) something like this: "I can't tell you to lie but if you want to state $79,000 on the income line, I will get you the loan". What do you think this borrower will do? The hard truth is, most mortgage brokers will say anything to get their commission, and most borrowers will lie to qualify for the loan. The loan officers at banks are also frequently under pressure to generate as many loans as they can.

In one case, I was told confidentially that a loan officer working at a major bank once suspected a borrower was lying and felt strongly that something seemed very wrong with the application. The officer reported it to a superior, but was told to ignore it because they are not required to verify income on a stated income loan. As long as *they* meet the Fannie Mae guidelines, the loan will be sold in the secondary market and they will have no risk. As a result, tens of billions of dollars of subprime mortgages were approved for people who did not have sufficient income to make the mortgage payments. This is why I called the subprime loans, "misstated income loans." Lenders seldom go after the borrower who "misstated" income on their applications for loan fraud because they themselves were willing participants to some extent, and they profited from these loans when they sold them to investors.

Recently, the Florida Attorney General was pursuing legal actions against some of the big banks for violation of the deceptive trade practices. He indicted Angelo Mozilo, the former CEO of Countrywide Financial Corp., for knowingly approving millions of dollars in loans to borrowers who could not afford the payments and then selling them to investors without full disclosure. Several former Countrywide employees were set to testify. On June 4, 2009, The Securities and Exchange Commission charged Mr. Mozilo with deception and fraud. Countrywide was the largest subprime mortgage lender, funding almost 20 percent of all toxic home loans. Countrywide also settled charges of lending abuse and consumer fraud brought by Attorney Generals of eleven states: California, Florida, Arizona, Connecticut, Iowa, Michigan, Illinois, North Carolina, Ohio, Texas and Washington. The settlement, valued at $8.4 billion, is the largest predatory lending settlement in history. The settlement required Countrywide (now acquired by Bank of America) to provide very generous loan modification terms and other relief to distressed borrowers. Many other major banks settled lawsuits out of court.

Creative Financing – Payment-Option, 2/28, 3/37 ARMs

If the "no doc, misstated income" loans were not toxic enough, lenders wanted to stretch loans to the bottom tier of subprime borrowers by adding creative financing practices. These borrowers typically would never have qualified to buy a house, but lenders created several new types of adjustable-rate mortgages (ARMs) or hybrid adjustable-rate mortgages such as Payment-option ARM, 2/28 ARM, 3/37 ARM, and convertible ARMs to get them qualified. Here are a few of the ARM loans that caused the most problems:

1. Payment-option ARM: This type of loan offers flexibility and choices that can be costly if the borrower is unable to refinance later. For a period of years specified in the mortgage, the borrower can choose the type of payment made each month.

Typically, there are four types of options:

(a) A minimum payment that does not cover interest – This option increases the total loan balance.

(b) An interest only payment that does not reduce the principal loan balance.

(c) A payment of interest and principal that pays off the mortgage in thirty years.

(d) A payment of interest and principal that pays off the mortgage in fifteen years.

After the option period, mortgage payments increase. In some cases, payments may increase before the option period ends. This happens when the borrower chooses to make only the minimum payments that do not cover the interest on the loan. The unpaid interest is added to the balance of the loan so the loan balance actually goes up instead of down. This is known as negative amortization, like a reverse mortgage (see chapter 24). When the loan balance reaches a certain specified amount, the payments will go up regardless of when the option period ends. Borrowers then must make significantly higher payments to lower the loan balance. Paying only minimum payments can increase the amount that is owed to a point where the borrower owes more than the home is worth, generally referred to as being "upside down" on the loan.

2. The 2/28 or 3/37 ARMs: These are the type of hybrid ARMs in which the rate is fixed at a higher rate than the fully indexed rate of regular ARMS for the first two or three years, then adjusts for each of the next 28 or 37 years to the value of a rate index at that time, plus a margin. This margin can be high, so the payment almost always goes up even if market rates are the same or lower. These loans often are offered to borrowers with

lower credit scores who may not qualify for a conventional loan. The idea is to give these borrowers two to three years to rebuild their credit and become eligible to refinance at a better rate.

3. Mortgages allowing interest-only payments: An interest-only option type of loan is typically available only for a limited time, after which payments go up sharply.

In general, these creative financing loans all offer lower interest, or lower payments in the initial years to help subprime borrowers to qualify, and then payment will increase substantially after two, three, five or ten years. The idea behind this is the hope that the borrowers will make more money or improve their credit scores later, so they can refinance the loan.

If the home value continued to increase, the problem would have resolved itself. But the bottom line is the lenders and mortgage brokers only cared about making more money and pushing the risk downstream to someone else. Many of these ARM loans are now faced with upward adjusting interest rates to as high as 10 percent to 12 percent. Borrowers holding this type of loan are the most vulnerable ones to default.

How Subprime Scam Artists Work – Case Study

Borrowers misstating their income and creative financing practices are not the only sources of subprime problems. In fact, one of the largest problems arising from subprime mortgages are loans fraudulently engineered by tens of thousands of scam artists all over the country. Even if homebuyers misstated their income to get their loans, most of them were legitimate buyers moving into homes, with every intention of making their mortgage payments. They may be stretched thin on a tight budget but they would do their best to keep their home. If home values continued to rise, the problem would have been better controlled. However, in the case of loan scam participants, those people never moved into the house. Those loans were in default shortly after the loan closings. I have first-hand information, because I personally encountered several scam artists myself in separate incidents over a two year period. Here is how a scam artist works:

He portrays himself as a representative of a group of investors wanting to buy houses for investment. He typically approaches sellers and home builders who have been unable to sell their homes for an extended period of time. He figures these sellers are more willing to offer huge discounts just to get their loans paid off (he also targets sellers who may have trouble making their mortgage payments). For example, a homebuilder has eight brand-new homes in his inventory, and he has been unable to sell them for a long time. Let's assume the sales price and market value of each of these homes is $500,000. The outstanding loan balances on these construction loans is $400,000 each (80 percent loan-to-value ratio). Since he is unable to sell these homes, they have tied up his capital and construction line-of-credit, prohibiting him from building more houses. He runs into cash flow problems, having to pay interest and taxes on so many unsold homes every month.

As his short-term construction loans approach the maturity dates, he is under a lot of pressure to get rid of these homes. Despite dropping his price to $450,000 each, no one buys. Then one day Mr. Scam Artist shows up at his door and quickly offers to buy all eight unsold houses from him at a price of $400,000 each (20 percent discount off the original prices). Without any hesitation, the homebuilder signs the contract, since the deal will save him from losing the houses to foreclosure. The buyers' names are purposely left blank on the contracts to allow Mr. Artist to fill in investor's names later. Even though the homebuilder will not make any money off the deal, nevertheless it will save him financially.

Next, Mr. Artist starts to search for innocent victims on the street, recruiting them to become his "investors". He offers people $20,000 each to participate in his genius "no-risk" investment plan, as long as the person has a credit score of 680 or above. He targets people like nurses, secretaries, or other low level workers living in apartments who he thinks can easily be lured with money. In our greedy society, he can probably find many people everyday. He tells the candidates that he has a brilliant idea to help them make quick money risk free. All they have to do is to become his investor, each buying one or more houses at the market value. He tells them he has lenders lined up to provide them all the loans needed and he has tenants lined up to lease all the houses, which will cover the mortgage payments fully. Not only do the investors not have to come up with a single penny, he will pay them $20,000 for each home they "buy", payable upfront at each closing. Since they are not paying more than the appraised values, it appears there is little or no risk. If the home values keep on going higher, they can expect to make more money down the road upon resale of the houses when the leases expired. Sounds like a real winning formula, right?

So, Mr. Scam Artist recruits two investors: both have relatively good credit scores, 720. Each investor will be required to buy four houses from the homebuilder mentioned earlier, at the original price of $500,000 each. He then takes the eight contracts signed by the homebuilder, fills in the buyer's names, changes each purchase price from $400,000 price to $500,000 (white out and copy), and has them signed by the two "investors".

Mr. Scam Artist then presents all eight contracts to his partner, a mortgage broker, to apply for eight mortgage loans from four different lenders. Each lender will process one loan for Investor A and one loan for Investor B, so neither of the two lenders will find out the borrower is buying more than one house. Since credit reports are typically updated no closer than thirty days apart, he makes sure all loans are processed and closed within a thirty-day window so lenders will not see a new mortgage debt showing up on the credit report while processing a loan. As we mentioned earlier, on stated income loans, lenders do not verify income. Therefore, Mr. Scam Artist or his mortgage broker partner will instruct the investors to fill in on the loan application whatever income amount is needed to qualify for the loan. In this case, they will ask the investors to put a very high income figure, hoping to get a 100 percent loan, or at least a 95 percent loan.

The mortgage broker orders appraisal reports from his "friendly" appraiser, who agrees to put a value on the high end of the range, which turns out to be $500,000 each, which just happens to match the purchase price. What a surprise! In many cases, the appraiser is a participant in the scam operation and falsifies a grossly inflated market value to make the numbers work.

Since income, appraisal, and credit scores all meet the qualifications, all four lenders approve the borrowers for a 95 percent loan at $475,000 each.

Shortly before closing, Mr. Artist goes back to the homebuilder and informs him that in order to make the figures work for the investor, he will have to mark up the purchase prices from $400,000 to $500,000 and use the surplus to cover down payments, closing costs and rents. The seller will still get his $400,000 agreed-upon price but all surpluses above $400,000 must be returned to the investor immediately upon funding at closing.

On the day of the first home closing, Mr. Scam Artist goes to a loan shark and borrows $25,000 hard money, at very high fees, for two days to cover the 5 percent down payment.

At closing, seller receives $500,000. Out of which $400,000 goes to repay his construction loan, and he returns the $100,000 surplus to Mr. Scam Artist. Mr. Artist immediately repays the $25,000 hard money loan (plus about $2,000 for two days of interest and fees), pays $20,000 to the investor, pays about $5,000 closing costs, and keeps about $48,000 for his "profit".

Then Mr. Scam Artist moves on to the second and subsequent closings until all eight houses are closed. Within thirty days, each investor made $80,000, and the scam artist made close to $390,000. Then, shortly after closing, the scam artist disappears. There are no tenants leasing the houses. The loans go into default almost immediately. The investors panic but are unable to locate the scam artist. Lenders foreclose on the houses and the credit records of the investors are ruined.

This is how scam artists work all over the country. Some of them wanting to do more deals before disappearing, would use part of their profit to make a few monthly mortgage payments before defaulting on the loans, just to make it less suspicious to the lenders and the investors while they are doing new deals. What makes these subprime mortgages far worse than others is that they started out upside down in loan-to-value ratio. When you have an appraisal showing the market value of the house at 125 percent of what it is really worth, and then the lender gives the borrower a 95 percent loan based on a good credit score and a stated income that is grossly exaggerated, it is essentially giving a loan of 119 percent LTV to a borrower who cannot afford to make a single payment. It's like a perfect storm!

Overall, these scam artists defrauded hundreds of millions of dollars from the banks off subprime loans in a short three to four years. As these scam operations spread across the country, lenders started to take legal actions against the borrowers (investors) for loan fraud and reported them to the Feds for criminal investigation. In one case against several investors and scam artists about four years ago, I was a federal expert witness and testified on behalf of the IRS and U.S. Attorney's Office. Several investors ended up in jail, but the scam artist was a fugitive and escaped to a foreign country. Although some of you may pity the investors recruited by the scam artists as victims, they are not. They were willing participants in the scam to defraud the banks and they pocketed a large sum of money that belonged to the banks. They willingly signed the promissory notes with personal guarantees. They also signed statements swearing that they would occupy the houses they were buying. How could they buy multiple houses within thirty days and swear that they intended to occupy all of them? They may be naive but they are not innocent.

For example, in one of the scam cases, a young single mother, a nurse, making slightly above minimum wage, was recruited by a scam artist to buy three expensive homes. She was very nervous at each closing, not sure if what she was doing was legal. Yet, she needed the money so she signed the documents at each closing and pocketed a quick $60,000, more than she could make in two years. When she found out later there was no one paying rent, she panicked. She wanted to sue the scam artist but he left the country when the U. S. Attorney's Office issued a warrant for his arrest. She wanted to sue the seller, but the seller never met her or took any of her money. The only participants who took money fraudulently were herself and the scam artist. She ended up in jail.

As loan defaults skyrocketed in 2008, the mortgage industry finally applied far more scrutiny to all loans. Despite that, for loans made in 2008, loan fraud grew 26 percent over 2007, according to the Mortgage Asset Research Institute. More than 60 percent of the mortgage loan fraud cases in 2008 stemmed from falsified applications, while 28 percent came from tax returns or financial statements, and 22 percent came from inflated appraisals from appraisers participating in the fraud.

Chapter 3: The Housing Bubble

Hundreds of billions of dollars of subprime loans were generated by lenders and sold to investors over a period of about six years. Most of the subprime borrowers ended up defaulting on their mortgages. Lenders then foreclosed on the houses and put them up for sale. Instead of collecting payments from the mortgages, the lenders ended up owning the houses. Before long, the market became flooded with foreclosed-home sales. Housing prices in many markets started to plummet in late 2007. Soon, lenders' problems rippled down to regular homeowners who were still paying their mortgages. This was the beginning of the long-anticipated burst of the housing bubble.

Financial Market Collapsed

In early 2008, foreclosures began getting out of control in several states, including California, Florida, Arizona, and Nevada. Today, these states now account for 46 percent of all foreclosures in the nation. Home values dropped an average of 31.1 percent nationally, with some markets dropping as much as 50 percent. Honest homeowners started to wonder why they were paying back their $300,000 mortgage while their house was now worth only $180,000. Since home values appear to continue heading down, they may be upside down in value for years to come. Many decided that it didn't make sense to continue paying, even though they could afford to. Many walked away from their house, causing default rates to rise around the country. The mortgage delinquency rate was 8.22 percent in the first quarter and 6.50 percent in the second quarter of 2009. To the investors who bought the CDO packages from the investment bankers, this means little or no money coming back. The investment bankers, on the other hand, are still holding on to billions of dollars of mortgages which now are becoming worthless, and no investors want to purchase any more CDO's. Investment bankers panicked because they borrowed billions of dollars in loans they are now unable to repay. Meanwhile, lenders are still holding on to billions of dollars of mortgages they are now unable to sell in the secondary market. As more and more mortgages are turning into worthless houses, banks are showing a depleted balance sheet. The whole financial system is frozen and many banks are going out of business. Many of the largest corporations in the country filed for bankruptcy protection, such as Lehman Brothers, Countrywide, Washington Mutual, IndyMac, Bank United FSB, Chrysler, General Motors, Extended Stay America, and Wachovia, just to name a few.. Many of the remaining major players, such as CIG, Bank of America, J. P. Morgan Chase, Citibank, Merrill Lynch, Fannie Mae, and Freddie Mac, were bailed out by the government or are being absorbed by other entities. Industry analysts estimate that the nation's banks are holding at least $2 trillion in troubled assets, which they are unable to dispose of.

The housing bubble has caused the stock market to tumble; the Dow Jones average lost more than 50 percent (from 14,164 points in October 2007 to below 6,470 points in March 2009), in less than eighteen months. The ripple effect spread all over the world. European and Asian markets dropped even more than U.S. markets. Russia's stock market has dropped about 80 percent in value. Overall, global stock markets combined have lost $21 trillion in value, and at one point, Americans have lost about $11 trillion of individual household wealth: $5.3 trillion in home equity losses and $5.7 trillion in stock market losses.

Unemployment Skyrocketed

Since the recession started in December 2007, 7.2 million non-farm jobs have been lost. 5.66 million of which were lost during the twelve month period from July 2008 through June 2009. The total number of unemployed has climbed to 14.7 million, and the unemployment rate shot up to 9.5 percent (national average) in June 2009, the highest rate since 1983 and more than double the 4.6 percent average rate just two years ago. If part-time and discouraged workers are factored in, the current unemployment rate would have surpassed 16 percent. In June 2009, sixteen states have unemployment rate exceeding 10 percent, such as California's 11.6 percent, Nevada's 12 percent, and Michigan's 15.2 percent, which is the highest in the nation. Job losses are wide spread, across all major industries, and continue at the rate of about 500,000 job losses per month. Another 2 million or more Americans are expected to lose their jobs in the coming months and the national average unemployment rate is projected to surpass 10 percent in early 2010.

Even in Texas, where the housing market was generally regarded as one of the healthiest markets in 2008, unemployment has grown rapidly to about 900,000. Another 300,000 Texans are expected to lose their jobs in 2009. The only somewhat "good" news, is that the number of national job losses may be declining. According to the U.S. Department of Labor statistics, preliminary figures showed 322,000 job losses in May 2009 and 467,000 job losses in June, 2009, as compared to 519,000 job losses in April 2009 and 652,000 job losses in March 2009. Still, it's too early to determine if this is a reliable trend.

Widespread Defaults and Foreclosures

The number of foreclosures skyrocketed to 2.2 million at the end of 2008, led by California, Florida, Arizona, and Nevada which accounted for 46 percent of foreclosures nationwide. By the first quarter of 2009, a record 5.4 million American homeowners were either late in payment or, already in foreclosure. According to figures released by Foreclosures.com, a new record of 175,199 homes were lost to foreclosure in March 2009, up 44 percent from February's record high of 121,756 homes. Overall, nearly 370,000 homes were reprocessed by lenders in the first quarter of 2009, compared to 266,986 in the last quarter of 2008 and 210,280 a year ago. These figures represent only the completed foreclosures. Through the first six months of 2009, foreclosures were up 9 percent over last year. Another 342,000 households received at least one foreclosure-related notice in April 2009, up 32 percent from a year ago, according to RealtyTrac. June 2009 was the fourth straight month with more than 300,000 households receiving foreclosure filings.

Therefore, contrary to some earlier reports indicating foreclosures may have bottomed out, foreclosures are still on the rise. It appears early this year, foreclosures were simply delayed by the temporary foreclosure freezes posted by major lenders, which expired in the first week of March 2009.

Even in better markets such as Texas, where foreclosure problems have been rather mild in comparison, there were nearly 100,000 foreclosures filed in 2008, and a far greater number is predicted in 2009, as indicated by one of highest percentage of extremely delinquent borrowers as reported by lenders. Houston, Texas, where the local economy was shielded by its strong energy sector, is also catching the flu, as oil and gas prices plummeted in early 2008, due to a sharp decline in demand. Therefore, while states like Texas may be among the last ones being dragged into the recession, they may be the last ones to get out as correction works its way through.

Subprime loans not only created the housing bubble, but they also triggered the biggest recession since the Great Depression of 1929! The Conference Board Consumer Confidence Index fell to an all time low of 26.9 percent in March 2009. Although the index has since improved to 40.8 percent in April and 54.9 percent in May, consumer confidence is still very unstable and can easily head back down with any bad news. In the following chapter, I will point out why the economy is likely to get worse before it gets better.

Chapter 4: When Will It Recover?

Twenty months into this deep recession, many of you are anxious to know how long it will take for the economy to recover. To begin with, let me first point out that as bad as everything has been, it's not even close to what happened during the Great Depression.

Comparing to the Great Depression

Here are a few notable statistics for comparison:

1. During the Great Depression, the U.S. gross domestic product (GDP) dropped by 32.6 percent, while GDP has dropped slightly under 4 percent in the current recession.
2. During the Great Depression, stocks dropped 80 percent, while stocks dropped about 50 percent at the lowest point in the current recession.

3. During the Great Depression, bank failures were about 40 percent, as compared to about 3 percent so far in this recession (granted, there are far more banks now).
4. During the Great Depression, the unemployment rate went up to 25.5 percent, while it stands at 9.5 percent as of June 2009.

Having said that, I do believe it is pre-mature for some economists to predict the current recession will be over by the fall of 2009. Understandably, the government is telling us things will be fine by the end of this year, because they are desperately trying to restore consumer confidence. We all hope they are correct; however, let's be more objective and try to analyze what is most likely to occur without being fooled by some news headlines. The most recent government report has already revised their earlier forecast of unemployment topping 9.5 percent. Now they are saying it will reach 10.1 percent and will remain at high level for several years. Many have questioned the earlier predictions by our government that the stimulus programs will generate three million jobs. Instead, we are still losing over 400,000 jobs each month. Only five states reported a decrease of unemployment rate in June 2009. Without question, the stimulus programs have helped saved many jobs. Did they prevent as many as three million people from losing their jobs? We will never know. When you are dealing with politicians, get used to seeing gray color instead of black or white.

The recent recovery of the Dow Jones average to the 9,300 level is much welcomed news. However, it is still 35 percent below the level before the current recession started. It is also doubtful if this rapid rising trend can be sustained in the near future. Part of the gain was attributed to many stocks in an over sold position in recent months and some rebound was predictable. Another part of the gain was attributed to companies cutting labor and other costs drastically to improve from previous dismal earnings. The third major part of the gain was attributed to companies beating earlier forecasts. When things were so bad last year, a lot of major companies charged off huge reserves for losses, particularly in the financial sector, and made very gloomy forecasts. Their strategy was that pushing a lot of bad news together has less negative impact than allowing releasing bad news over a long period of time. For example, if XYZ Company reported a loss of $300 million in one quarter (by charging off large amount for loss reserves) and then showed making $25 million, $50 million, and $75 million profit in subsequent quarters, its stock is likely to produce a sizable gain, despite a net loss of $150 million over the past four quarters. On the other hand, if the company reported $35 million losses in each of the four quarters, its stocks would likely suffer a sizable loss, even though the net loss of $140 million for the year is smaller. The market tends to focus on current growth, how it compares to estimates, and forgives older problems. Therefore, when companies made gloomy forecasts and then "beat" the estimates, the stock market reacted favorably, even though the companies still showed a decline in sales or earnings. Therefore, it is essential to keep in mind the basic fundamentals of stock values: earnings, profits, and sales. If the stocks go up because companies are making more money than the same period a year ago, then it will likely to sustain. Otherwise, if the gains were manipulated by simply beating lower estimates, or resulted from a non-recurring event, it will not sustain.

For example, Goldman Sacks beats all estimates by reporting a record second quarter earnings of $3.44 billion. Analysts attributed part of the success to less competition because many of its rivals have gone out of business. On the other hand, Goldman Sachs borrowed $10 billion from the federal Troubled Asset Relief Program (TARP) money for virtually nothing, and then lending it out at a 3 to 4 percentage point markup, which accounted for a good part of the earnings. They are making huge profit off government subsidy. In addition, according to a government report, out of the $170 billion that the government spent to rescue AIG, $13 billion actually flowed to Goldman, AIG's biggest trading partner. These are non-recurring win-fall profits that will not show in the next quarter.

By definition, the end of a recession occurs when there is two consecutive quarters of positive GDP growth. Although the downward trend of the GDP is easing, we are still in a negative territory. We have yet to see the first quarter of positive GDP growth. Therefore, at the very least, we are two quarters away from the end of the recession. It is important to point out that the end of recession only means we have reached the bottom. You will not feel a huge difference between negative 0.1 percent and positive 0.1 percent GDP. Only politicians and the media will make a big deal out of a merely 0.2 percent change. It will hardly put more money in your pocket. To be realistic, the economy is likely to stay near the bottom throughout 2010, and begin a real growth in 2011.

Another Wave of Problems Coming?

Here are some of the major concerns:

1. More Foreclosures: There are still more adjustable rate mortgages due for recast in 2009, 2010, and 2011. When payments jump, many borrowers will not be able to make the new payments. Between 65 percent and 75 percent of the completed loan modifications are likely to redefault, according to a report issued by the credit-rating agency Fitch Ratings. This is because lenders were unwilling to give significant concessions in the early months of this crisis. Most loan modifications completed last year were based on the HomeSaver Advance, a loss mitigation program offered by Fannie Mae. All that

program did was offer borrowers an unsecured personal loan to replace all delinquent mortgage payments, interest, taxes, insurance, and late fees. The loan was set at 5 percent interest, with no interest and no payment for the first 6 months. This means their mortgage payments were not reduced, and they actually went up after the initial six months. It is estimated that only 42 percent of loans modified in 2008 resulted in reduced monthly payments for borrowers. The redefault of modified loans will keep foreclosures at a high level in the coming months. In fact, California's foreclosure filings are still running at 80,000 to 90,000 per month; that is one every 30 seconds! A new California Foreclosure Prevention plan was implemented by the state, beginning June 15, 2009, which froze all foreclosures for ninety days. This lowered the total foreclosure filings in the nation temporarily, but they will jump up again in mid-September. Many local and state agencies have also implemented measures to delay foreclosures. But unless the delinquent loans are modified or refinanced, the foreclosures are simply delayed. Since late 2008, lenders became more aggressive in offering loan modification concessions. Therefore, those loan modifications completed since October 2008, with higher reduction in payments, will have a far greater chance of success. Lenders have also stepped up on their offering of short sales, which will certainly reduce the number of future foreclosure filings.

2. Drastic increase in credit card defaults: As job losses continue at the pace of 500,000 a month, more and more consumers will live on their credit cards. Soon, credit card defaults will hit the lenders hard. According to the Federal Reserve, total U.S. revolving debts is now over $850 billion. You can just imagine the impact on the financial institutions if credit card defaults

begin to follow the trend of the mortgage defaults. In chapter 20, I will cover more of this topic.

3. Drastic increase in commercial loan defaults: Retailers are suffering from slow sales, and many are going out of business. Even major shopping malls are filing for bankruptcy, as fewer people are shopping. The global recession also slowed down exports to the lowest level in three years. Car dealerships are closing, as the auto makers are in deep trouble. Manufacturers are closing down industrial plants or reducing their industrial space. Hotels are full of empty rooms, as people have reduced their leisure travel. Apartment owners are hurting, as tenants are unable to make rent payments or move back with their parents to cut expenses. All in all, commercial loan defaults are expected to trigger the next round of major foreclosures, which in turn will dampen the recovery of the financial markets. One commercial loan default could equal hundreds of home loan defaults. A New York City commissioner told the City Council Community Department Committee in May 2009 that as many as 90,000 of the city's apartments were in danger of foreclosures. These are mostly run down apartments purchased by private equity firms at the top of the market. Now with the property values dropping significantly, these investment companies are looking to cut their losses, displacing many of the renters as a result. As a result, Fannie Mae recently launched its so-called Real Estate Owned Rental Policy, which gives tenants of foreclosed properties the option to accept new month-to-month rental agreements. Such a program will help the renters but, most importantly, it will also bring some much needed cash flow for the lenders. While there is almost zero credit available for any commercial loans at this time, major banks are beginning to consider commercial loan modifications

on a case by case basis. Banks will continue to hurt through 2010, but the government bailout thus far has prevented more major banks from failing. Having said that, the government did recently turn down New York based CIT Group for more bailout money. It is unclear what the government will do if the financial institutions are hit with larger than expected commercial loan defaults. The government is working on incentive programs to help investors acquire toxic assets from the banks' balance sheets. If this is successful, banks will then be able to free up their capital, and then they can see the light at the end of the tunnel, probably in 2011.

4. Slow implementation of government's stimulus programs: The government has announced numerous aggressive economic Stimulus programs. Some are short term but many are long-terms projects, such as high-speed rails, scientific research that will have virtually no impact on getting the economy back on track. In addition, due to typical government red tape, and oversight obstacles, only a small portion of the Stimulus money had been funded as of June 2009. A lot of the early $700 billion, TARP money to bail out major banks was wasted because the programs were created in a rush before oversight safeguards were implemented. There were allegations that some of the $170 billion bailout money to AIG ended up in huge bonuses to its executives. Many of the banks received the federal aid to support increased lending have instead used some of the money to make investments, repay debts, or buy other banks. Even today, the Treasury Department has not taken steps to require all TARP recipients to report on their actual use of funds. Therefore, even if it slows down the application of the stimulus funding, a good oversight system is important to make sure our government does not simply hand out money

everywhere and end up wasting it, without achieving what it was originally intended. If the federal aid is aimed at stimulating more lending, then those funds should be restricted for such purpose. So far, our government has spent a total of $3 trillion (out of $4.7 trillion commitment) from about 50 initiatives and programs to help the financial sector through its crisis.

All this means the recovery may be slower than some may think. The economy shrank at the pace of 6.3 percent in the fourth quarter of 2008 and by another 5.7 percent in the first quarter of 2009. That was the worst six month performance in fifty years. While the preliminary figure showed GDP shrank by only 1.0 percent in the second quarter of 2009, it is still too soon to assume the third quarter of 2009 will show a GDP gain.

How Soon Will Home Values Recover?

Regarding the housing market, foreclosures and foreclosure notices continue to rise at a record pace. As more and more homeowners are choosing loan modifications, refinancing, or short sales, the number of foreclosures will level off by early 2010. Many of the foreclosed homes will end up in the hands of bargain investors. At some point, these investors will have to unload these investment houses, which will flood the market with more housing inventory. Therefore, it is safe to assume a buyer's market will continue in the upcoming years.

In order for home values to recover, home sales must first pick up. Unfortunately, there are so many barriers preventing that from happening. Aside from having to compete with foreclosure sales, regular sellers are unable to sell their homes because very few buyers are able to obtain mortgage loans, unless they have ample amount of money for a down payment. To make things worse, lenders have tightened their appraisal guidelines and are engaging only their most conservative appraisers. As a result, many sales are lost when the appraised value falls below contract prices.

Millions of Americans have had their credit ruined by foreclosures, credit card defaults, or bankruptcies. Such serious adverse events stay on a borrower's credit report for at least seven years (see chapter 31). According to Fannie Mae's latest guidelines, five years time must be passed from the date of a foreclosure sale completion before a new loan application can be considered. In the case of a chapter 13 bankruptcy (see chapter 29) on record, either two years from the discharge date or four years from the dismissal date must be passed. For all other bankruptcies, four years from either the discharge or dismissal date must be passed. For multiple bankruptcy filings, five year period from most recent bankruptcy dismissal or discharge date must be passed before Fannie Mae will accept new loan application. Therefore, most of this large group of people will not be qualified for a loan to buy a home again in the next four to seven years. After four to five years, we can reasonably expect to see a large increase of homebuyers re-entering the market, thus setting a beginning of a sustained rise in home values. However, for home values to return to the high levels prior to the current housing bubble, it will likely take at least seven years, possibly longer. Remember, if home values have dropped by 50 percent, it will take a 100 percent increase to return to the old level. Just do your math! It will take ten years of an average gain of 10 percent per year to increase by 100 percent.

When Will the Job Market Recover?

In order for the economy to recover, it has to start with jobs. In order for the job market return to net gains, companies will have to return to profitable and growth. Almost all previous recessions started with significant job losses, and almost all previous recoveries started with significant job gains. Therefore, in order to start our recovery this time, we must see new jobs being added, instead of declining. Even if the economy reaches the bottom and job losses level off, this does not mean companies will go out and start hiring immediately. As long as companies are losing money, it is unlikely that we will see any significant new hiring. I am amazed to see the media, and the stock market, jump up and celebrate the "good" news that "only" 322,000 jobs were lost in May 2009. It kind of gives you a perspective of how bad things really are. The hard truth is, we are still losing jobs. A recovery means gaining jobs, not losing fewer jobs! Based on most predictions, at least another 2 million job losses are expected and the nation's unemployment rate is likely to hit double digits by the early 2010.

Most likely, job losses will bottom out by the first quarter of 2010 and stay close to the bottom for the rest of 2010. Recovery in 2011 is a more likely scenario than a recovery this year or early next year, which many are predicting. Keep in mind that even if the current recession has reached a bottom, this does not mean a recovery is imminent. Many times in the past, there were several "false recoveries" or minor upticks that were not sustained. Early this year, headlines such as "Foreclosures are coming down" or "Home sales recover" turned out to be far premature. They failed to tell you that foreclosures were frozen under a temporary moratorium, and home sales were up due largely to bargain hunters buying foreclosure sales or taking advantage of the first-time homebuyer's tax credit.

The bottom line is, the media and most economists are frequently caught up in a debate trying to determine whether we are in a recession or out of a recession. A recession is not an event like going to a funeral, whereby after they bury the dead, it's over and you go on with your daily life. It takes years of things going wrong to fall into a recession and it usually takes years of doing many things right to get out of a recession. Our government is doing a lot to stabilize the financial market. However, there is no magic wand that anyone can wave to turn paper into money. It will take time, and the economy should resume slow growth by the second half of 2010. Once the market turns the corner, our government's top priority must focus on implementing far more strict guidelines (to prevent a future recurrence of events we covered in chapter 1) and dealing with the runaway deficit crisis. This housing bubble is a lesson to learn and a lesson to teach our next generations.

Chapter 5: Loan Modification

Loan Modification, mortgage modification, loan arbitration, loan mitigation, and loss mitigation are various names used for the same purpose: to change the terms of an existing loan. The aim of a loan modification is to enable the mortgagor (borrower) to pay off the loan in the foreseeable future and, most importantly, to avoid a foreclosure. Always keep in mind that just because you turn in an application for a loan modification, it does not stop the legal process of foreclosure. Therefore, I recommend that you start your loan modification early and do not wait until the foreclosure process has already started. In order for your lender to approve a loan modification, it will first determine whether it will be better off negotiating a reduced mortgage payment with you than foreclosing on your home. In the following chapters, I will show you how lenders do their analysis and what you need to do to get approval for a loan modification.

How Loan Modification Can Help You

Loan modification will result in lower mortgage payments for the borrower by one or more of the following changes made on an existing loan:

1. Lowering the interest rate of an existing loan
2. Extending the paying term over more years
3. Converting an adjustable rate mortgage or an interest-only loan to a fixed loan with lower interest
4. Changing a thirty year amortization to a forty year amortization
5. Forbearance -- skipping one or more payments
6. Principal reduction
7. Repayment plan -- spread out past-due payments over many months

Most loan modifications do not involve closing fees, legal fees, surveys, or inspections. While an appraisal is not required, lenders do order a Broker's Price Opinion (BPO) to help them determine the amount of equity in your home. In the following chapters, I will help you understand all the components that directly or indirectly affect your chance of getting your loan modified by your lender. There is no uniform standard set by lenders. Each lender has its unique situation, and some may be more eager to negotiate than others. For example, those banks that bought assets from defunct lenders at 40 cents on the dollar are able to grant you far more generous reductions and still make a profit. In addition, since most loans are owned by investors, each investment pool may set its own bottom line, which may be quite different from others. Chapter 18 will give you many case studies of what major lenders have approved so far on loan modifications and what their general guidelines are. Before I get into those details, you need to first understand how lenders work and what they are dealing with.

Few people had heard of the term "loan modification" prior to December 2007. Most banks used to keep just a couple of people in their loss mitigation department because they were used to dealing with just a handful of cases when a borrower suffered extreme hardship. The banking system was set up so that they simply were unable to allow loan payments to be reduced, except in some extreme hardship cases, when they would agree to modify the repayment in such a way that the borrower could then afford to make payments. In the past, when a borrower was late in payments, the lenders simply proceeded with foreclosure. Bankers operate by the book, with rules set by Fannie Mae, Freddie Mac, and investors. As I discussed in chapter 1, most mortgage lenders are nothing more than retail outlets originating loans in the primary market. Then they sell most of the mortgages to Fannie Mae and Freddie Mac in the secondary market which, in turn, sell them in large pools to investors. The local lender you are dealing with makes money off the interest spread and fees. The mortgage loans are mostly serviced by a third- party managing entity on behalf of investors, although some major lenders may retain the servicing in-house. Your mortgage loan can easily be owned by the Bank of China and serviced by a company in India.

Therefore, the system makes it almost impossible for lenders to handle a large influx of loan modification demands. When home values tumble down, lenders are either going out of business or running out of money. In the fourth quarter of 2008, at the urging of Congress, many major banks passed a temporary moratorium to halt all new foreclosures temporarily until the first week of March 2009, in order to give them time to work with Congress and their investors for a possible solution. As a result, Congress, lenders and their investors have all determined that they are much better off renegotiating the payment terms of existing borrowers to keep them in the house than adding more foreclosures to a market already flooded with foreclosures. Congress followed by providing $75 billion of dollars of incentives to help lenders that are willing to refinance or modify loans to help troubled borrowers. Unfortunately, these new Obama Administration programs (see chapter 13) have a lot of restrictions and many troubled homeowners will not qualify. As of mid-July 2009, only about 200,000 borrowers were enrolled in the three-month trial loan modifications.

As I mentioned in chapter 4, in most of the loan modifications done in early 2008 or before, lenders did not give any significant concessions to borrowers. As a result, a large percentage of the modified loans redefaulted and ended up in foreclosure. Lenders did not foresee such a scenario coming, and it created a new wave of foreclosures. It became so bad California had to freeze all foreclosures again, starting June 15, 2009, for ninety days in order to give the lenders more time to process more aggressive loan modifications. The crisis is so serious there is simply no magic wand that can turn things around overnight. To make things worse, the process is further slowed down by many other problems. Homeowners needing help are caught in a sea of confusion. I will cover these problems and the qualifications of loan modification in the following chapters.

How Does a Bank's Loss Mitigation Department Work?

For years, the loss mitigation department of most lenders used to employ just a few people. Now, that department has become the busiest department in the lending industry. Lenders have no choice but to move employees from other departments into the loss mitigation department. Most of these staff members lack proper training. To some degree, even the management executives are learning on the job because nothing like this ever happened before. Each loss mitigator or negotiator is handling 350 to 450 files at one time, and some of them are running about three months behind. To make things worse, most borrowers jamming the phones, asking for loan modifications, have no idea what they are supposed to do, or what documents are required in order to qualify for payment reduction. The loan negotiators do not have the time, or the incentive, to teach each person on the phone how to get their loan modified or whether they are qualified. Many of the loan negotiators earn a relatively low salary (median annual salary is about $43,000), with an incentive bonus measured by the number of files they successfully close in a month. In the case of short sales, they get an extra bonus if they close a deal above a certain level based on percentage of recovery (bank's return of investment).

These mitigators work for the banks, and their primary interest is to either make money for the banks or, in this case, lose less money. Therefore, they have very little incentive to spend a lot of time teaching you how to get the best deal for you. As a result, without proper knowledge, most borrowers requesting a loan modification directly from their lenders end up rejected, or placed at the bottom of the pile due to an incomplete package or because they are simply not qualified. Some may be told, "Your file is waiting for the investor's approval," which is usually not true. Investors typically hold a tiny percentage of ownership of a large pool of mortgages. They do not get involved in the decision of whether to approve your single loan modification. Typically, either your bank's senior management or an officer of the pool servicing company is going to make the final decision. Realistically, once your file is completed, the final approval or rejection takes less than 15 minutes.

The key of success is to learn how to do it right and present a complete package to your lender the first time. It will save you (and the lender) time, money, and possibly your home. Keep in mind that in most cases, your lender will lose more money if it forecloses on your home. Your lender does want to work with you to modify your loan for mutual benefits if you are qualified. Due to the overwhelming requests, it just doesn't have the time to teach you step by step. For a loan modification to work, you and your lender must structure a win-win situation for both parties. You are looking for a way to reduce your mortgage payment to save your home and your lender is looking for a way to avoid losing more money in a foreclosure if you walk away. Loan modification is not a rocket science. If you follow the steps carefully in the following chapters, you can successfully submit your own loan modification application meeting your lender's requirements. Keep in mind, it is a time-consuming process to do a loan modification, and not all loans can be modified. Troubled homeowners may have heard about bailout programs, with new terminologies. Quite frankly, most people are confused and live under a cloud of uncertainty.

Loan Modification Present Value Test

Your lender will consider modifying your loan to allow you to reduce your mortgage payment if it believes it will lose more money foreclosing on your home than the concessions it will give you in a loan modification. All lenders will run their own Present Value Test to determine whether they will even consider you for a loan modification. In chapter 10, I will point out that most lenders order a Broker's Price Opinion (BPO), from a real estate broker to determine the current market value of your home. In chapter 11, I will show you that the typical net proceeds to the lender from a REO (foreclosed Real Estate Owned by lender) sale is between 75 percent to 80 percent of the market value, after deducting about 7 percent for sales expenses and another 15 percent for marketing and legal fees, utilities, property taxes, insurance, maintenance, repairs, distress sale discounts, and so on. If your loan-to-value (LTV) ratio is 70 percent or below, your lender will not even consider you for a loan modification, because it does not believe it will lose any money by foreclosing on your home. 70 percent to 75 percent LTV ratios fall within the borderline where your lender may or may not accept loan modification. Generally speaking, 78 percent LTV ratio is considered the breakeven point whereby your lender is expected a 100 percent loan recovery.

For example, you purchased your home for $400,000 four years ago. You had a 90 percent loan of $360,000, at the interest rate of 7 percent, thirty-year fixed, with a monthly payment of $2,395 (principal and interest). Your current loan balance is $343,700. Now you have suffered a hardship (see chapter 14), resulting in a deficit in your budget (see chapter 15) and are unable to continue making the mortgage payment. The current market value of your home has dropped from $400,000 to $340,000 (LTV ratio is now 101 percent). This means your house is worth about the same as what you owe so you would prefer to keep your home rather than letting it be foreclosed by your lender which will hurt your credit score significantly (see chapter 31). If your lender proceeds with foreclosure, it will expect to net about $265,200 ($340,000 less 22 percent), which is well below your current loan balance. Thus, your lender will be more than willing to modify your loan as long as the Present Value of the modified loan will result in a greater amount than $262,200 to them. As for you, if you end up with lower payments without adding to your balance, you get something for nothing! A win-win compromise!

For comparison, let me help you calculate a present value in a simplified way without getting too confusing. Let's assume your lender is willing to reduce your 7 percent fixed interest rate to 3 percent the first year, 4 percent the second year, 5 percent the third year, and then fixed at 5.5 percent the fourth year for the duration of your loan, reamortized over thirty years. Your mortgage payment (principal and interest) will be reduced to $1,518 the first year, $1,719 the second year, $1,933 the third year, and then $2,044 the fourth and remaining years. If your lender applies a four year projection of your modified loan (assuming you will sell your home or refinance at the end of four years), the estimated total amount it will receive at the end of four years (FV-4 = future value in year 4) is: $343,700 (present value) x 1.03 (after one year) x 1.04 (after two years) x 1.05 (after three years) x 1.055 (after four years) = $407,842 (future value, compounded annually).

Now, if you discount the future value backward at the original loan interest rate of 7 percent per year: $407,842 (future value in year 4) x 0.93468 (1/1.07 end of year 3) x 0.93468 (1/1.07 end of year 2) x 0.93468 (1/1.07 end of year 1) x 0.93468 (1/1.07 present) = $311,275 (PV). This is the Present Value of your modified loan as compared to $343,700 without the loan modification, and the estimated $262,200 net if your lender proceeds with foreclosure. Under this scenario, it will work perfectly for both parties. You, the borrower, will get your first-year payment reduced by $877 a month to help you balance your budget and keep your home. Your lender, despite giving you $32,425 of concession in present value, will still be $49,075 better than proceeding with a foreclosure. Although lenders may apply a different discount rate or year, this present value test is what all lenders use to determine if they will consider your request for a loan modification. In conclusion, this is a classic example of how a loan modification should work. In the following chapters, I will teach you how to prepare your loan modification package so it is acceptable to your lender. Before I get into that, I would like to caution you about some of the problems associated with loan modifications.

Loan Modification – Commercial Loans

For commercial loans, there are no fixed guidelines or rules. Perhaps the only rule you need to follow is that do not be afraid to ask. Most lenders are now willing to negotiate and modify commercial loans to avoid a foreclosure. To some degree, the basic guidelines for home loan modifications will apply to commercial loan modifications. Lenders will consider lowering your monthly payment by reducing interest rates in the short term or re-amortize over longer years. The bottom is the same, your lender must believe that the present value of a loan modification will result in a higher amount than if they proceed with foreclosure. The key is going to be the current market value. Since commercial properties range from retail centers, office buildings, to multi-family complexes and industrial properties, the market condition for each type or each location can vary greatly. Again, if you have 30% or more in equity based on current market value, your lender will probably be better off to foreclose. It is likely they will recover most of not all of the outstanding debts. If you had signed personal guarantee on your commercial property, your lender will first putting pressure on you to sell your assets to pay the borrower's shortage. Therefore, unlike home loans, lenders will look at each commercial loan modification on a case-by-case basis. If there are several guarantors on the note, they will first explore the possibility of recovering shortfalls from the guarantors. If that is not available, then they will engage into serious negotiation on your commercial loan. Commercial loans are being monitored closely by federal bank examiners once or twice a year. Unlike home mortgage loans, commercial borrowers are required to submit current financial statements, tax receipts, insurance certificates, personal financial statements from guarantors no less than once a year. Therefore, if you are unable to make your loan payments, your lender will need some explanation of your hardship. In most cases, your loan will be transferred into the work-out department so your "friendship" relationship with your loan officer will go down the drain. Most banks want to avoid any emotional feeling between the loan officer and you when you are in trouble.

Chapter 6: How to Avoid Scam Artists

The possibility of losing your home to foreclosure can be terrifying, and the reality that scam artists are preying on the vulnerability of desperate homeowners is equally frightening. Due to the fact that there are millions of homeowners needing help to get their loan payments reduced in order to keep their homes, loan modification suddenly becomes the biggest new industry.

How Scam Artists Operate?

Almost overnight, there are tens of thousands of loan modification consultants or "foreclosure experts" appearing, and many of them are scam operations. Originated mostly from California and Florida where foreclosures dominated, these so called loan modification consultants or foreclosure rescue firms use a variety of tactics to find homeowners in distress. Some search foreclosure notices through public files at local county offices, and then send personalized letters or E-mails to homeowners. Others take a broader approach through ads on the

Internet, on television, or in the newspaper, posters on telephone pole, flyers at your door, etc. In a short few months, their operations have expanded to all over the country. The scam artists use simple straightforward messages, like "We guarantee to stop your foreclosure", "We can Save your Home, Guaranteed. Free Consultation", or "We have special relationship inside the lenders to stop your foreclosure". Interestingly, these may be the same scam artists who started the sub-prime loan frauds a few years ago which caused the housing bubble and are now advertising to "save your home"! It has become so bad that the Federal Trade Commission has issued numerous warnings on loan modification or foreclosure "rescue" solicitations from bogus websites, direct mails, Emails or even cold callings. Their direct mails often appear to come from your lender offering to lower your mortgage payments. Some are brazen enough to offer you a money-back guarantee. Unfortunately, once these foreclosure fraudsters take your money, usually from $2,000 to $3,000, they leave you in the cold. Amazingly, the competition among the scam artists became so keen that some even offer you a discounted fee, as low as $795. Just imagine, you can get a scam discount! Does it make you feel any better? In the worst cases, some of them even assume ownership of your property by deceiving you. They make you think you are signing documents for a new loan to help you make your existing mortgage current. This is a trick; you are actually signing the title of your house to the scam artist in exchange for a "rescue" loan. Then when it's too late to save your home, they take the property or steal the equity of your home. Others may use the personal data you gave them to steal your identity for more damages.

Top Ten Rules on How to Avoid Scams

The best rules to avoid scammers are:

1. Deal locally with folks you know or you can meet in person;
2. Do not send your personal confidential information to strangers;
3. Only a scammer will "guarantee" saving your home;
4. Leaders typically do not send you unsolicited offer to lower your existing mortgage payments unless you are delinquent on your payments or if it comes directly from government's Making Home affordable program;
5. Do not send money to total strangers by mail or through Internet before they perform any service;
6. Scam Artists' websites typically do not show a street office address where you may visit in person. Either they do not show any street address or the list only a P.O. Box address. As you can expect, scammers do not want to be found. In fact, many of them do not even show a phone number. They typically call you from a cell phone once you signed up on line. Many scammers change their name, phone, and address constantly.
7. Scam Artists also change company names and their website domain names all the time. The only reason a company changes its name all the time is to get away from scams being caught. You may find a new website that has a different name but the format and design is usually the same as the one you have seen before. This is because it costs just a few dollars to get a new domain name and forward it to the same website as compared to the cost of designing new web pages. So, it is prudent to do

some research and deal only with companies that have been in business for many years under the same name.

8. If you are renting a house, make sure the person showing you the house is either the listing Realtor or the owner (or an owner's representative). If you do not have a Realtor representing you, then check the county tax record, enter the property address, you should be able to find the owner's name. Make sure if you do sign a lease and pay the first month rent and one month deposit, the check is made payable to the owner's name. Otherwise, you may be writing a check to a scam artist who has nothing to do with the house or the listing agent. These types of scam artists actually work in person and they target people looking to rent a house. First the scam artist found vacant houses for rent with a Realtor's lockbox. Somehow they managed to get the key from the lockbox and made a duplicate key. Then they solicit people looking to rent a house and offer them a great deal if they sign a lease immediately. Once you fall for it, then they will ask you to give them first month rent plus deposit, payable to a name who he claims is the "owner". Once you do that, he will give you the key and tell you feel free to move in any time. Guess what, this guy has nothing to do with the owner or the listing Realtor. You just gave away two months rent money to a scam artist on a phony lease! Before you write the rent check, try asking for an original copy of a utilities bill to determine the cost of utilities. Original utilities bill should show the name and address same as the landlord's name on your lease agreement. A scam artist will not be able to produce you any original utility bill from that address. This type of scam operation is getting more popular since more and more home buyers are unable to obtain a loan so they resort to leasing or lease/purchase a home.

9. There is another popular scam operation which has nothing to do with homes. If you are selling something on eBay or Craigslist, a common scam is someone pretending he is a buyer, sending you a cashier's check for his purchase. The check turns out to have an amount far more than what he is supposed to pay. He blames it on a dumb mistake and asks you to send him the overpaid portion. As it turns out, his cashier's check is fake and not only that you lost your product, you also lost the money you send to the scam artist. Therefore, if you run into such a case, just make sure the cashier's check is good before you release the product or send the overpaid money. If someone sends you more money than he should, beware and report to the authorities. A similar scam would lead you to believe that someone has a large sum of money coming from Africa wanting to share with you.... Whatever forms this scam may come, just do not send any of your money out.
10. Check with the Better Business Bureau for complaints filed against the entity you are dealing. You can also look up www.RipoffReport.com

If you think you have been a victim of the foreclosure or loan modification fraud, contact the Federal Trade Commission or your state Attorney General. FBI currently has nearly 2,350 mortgage fraud scam cases, almost 400 percent increase from five years ago. If you paid with your credit card, try to file a dispute with your credit card company. They may be able to help you reverse that charge if caught early.

Chapter 7: Loan Modification Consultants

I do like to point out that not all loan modification solicitations are scams. There are many legitimate consultants who can help you process your loan modification or short sales if you are unable to process it yourself.

Should You Engage a Loan Modification Consultant?

Although there are many loan modification consultants offering legitimate help, a great majority of them are merely "lead generators". Many of these so-called consultants solicit your business through Emails, mails and phone calls know very little about processing loan modification or short sales. All they do is working on the marketing side to generate leads, and then they will send the leads to legitimate professional loan modification processing companies. They simply make a commission or a mark-up fee as their profit. In most cases, the real professional consultants will take over the file and deal with you directly. In some cases, you may continue to work through the lead generating "consultant" who you contacted originally. Typical fees charged for a turnkey loan modification processing are from $2,000 to $3,000, out of which the lead generator makes about $500 to $1,000. The loan modification process does involve a lot of time and work so the fees are somewhat justified if you don't have the time nor desire to do it yourself. However, for a homeowner who is already struggling to meet his mortgage payment, $2,000 to $3,000 is a lot of money, even if it is not a scam operation. Keep in mind there is no guarantee your lender will approve your modification. Even if they do, your savings may end up below the fees you are paying the consultant. On the other hand, many homeowners do end up saving tens of thousands of dollars which would have justified the high fees. Most people will be better off learning everything from this book and then process your own loan modification or short sale without spending a lot of money on a consultant.

What Does Your Lender Think?

All lenders prefer to deal directly with the borrower without going through a third party. They believe the money you are paying a third party consultant can be paid to them instead. After all, if you are telling your lender you are short of money to make existing mortgage payment, they will be wondering how you come up with thousands of dollars to engage a consultant? Also, for confidentiality and liability reasons, your lender will almost always send documents and correspondences directly to you instead of sending to your consultant. Just imagine, each time you received any documents from your lender, you have to send them to the lead generating consultant who in turn will forward them to the loan modification processing company. There is going to be a lot of time loss, if not mails loss. If you do not have the time or the ability to process your own loan modification or short sale with your lender, then I suggest you to engage a consultant in your local area where you can meet in person and work through the process together.

There is one advantage of engaging a third party to negotiate with your lender on your behalf. You, the borrower, are typically more emotional in stressful times and there is a tendency you may lose your temper and start yelling at the person on the phone if things are not moving along as quickly as you would like. If you do that, you will be inviting a rejection or being pushed to the bottom of the stack. Also, even if you managed to get close to the end of the process, you may jump on whatever first reduction offer your lender throws at you. An experienced professional negotiator may hold out for a far better modification than you will.

In general, borrowers who are behind in their payments will be considered a higher priority from the lenders than those continue making timely payments. While we can understand the logic behind such unwritten rules, it could backfire on the lenders. Many loan modification consultants are asking their clients not to make their loan payments on purpose in order to manipulate the system and gain advantage of getting their files processed faster or pushing for a better deal, even if their clients can afford the payments. Falling behind in loan payments will adversely affect your credit score and stay on your credit report (see chapter 31) for seven years. We do not recommend anyone not to make loan payments on purpose. As shown in chapter 18, not all lenders require payment late before considering a loan modification.

Chapter 8: HUD Counseling Centers

There are many non-profit counseling centers sponsored or approved by HUD to help homeowners. These counseling sessions are either free or low cost. You can call 1-888-995-HOPE to locate a counseling center in your area. You can also search for a counselor in your area on the Web sites of either the National Foundation for Credit Counseling or the Association of Independent Consumer Credit Counseling Agencies.

What Can You Expect to Learn From Counseling Centers?

The primary function of the counselors at these counseling centers is to point out to you all the options you may have besides foreclosure or filing for bankruptcy. Based on the income you stated, they may be able to lead you in the right direction. As you can expect during this troubled times, lines could be very long at these centers. Do not expect these counselors to spend hours working on one case to help you figure out what you can afford. They will simply walk you through all the options you may have, and what documents you may need to prepare. Many non-profit counseling centers are funded by creditors. They will advise you to do whatever you can, such as getting a second job, in order to avoid a foreclosure or filing for bankruptcy which will hurt the creditors (and you) the most.

List of Government Websites that Can Help You

Most of the information they will provide you are available on various public websites such as:

www.HopeNow.com

www.FannieMae.com

www.FreddieMac.com

www.MakingHomesAffordable.gov

www.HUD.gov

While these Websites, as well as the HUD counseling centers, will provide you a lot of useful information regarding many options available to you, this book goes much farther to show you how to prepare your package that will meet your lender's requirements. It will educate you not only to what options you may have, but how to write your hardship letter, how to structure your budget, where to submit your package, check list of everything you need to prepare, what to expect from the lenders, and many other related topics that every homeowner should know.

Chapter 9: Home Equity

Home ownership has and always will be part of the American Dream. In the past decades, home equity has been a life saver for most Americans who suffered financial hardship. When nothing else works, most people in financial difficulties often resort to their home equity for relief, either by selling their home to cashing out their home equity, or by borrowing more through home equity loans or refinancing. Unfortunately, their luck has run out. The home equity safe haven has all but vanished. Across the country, home values have dropped an average of 31.1 percent. According to the Wall Street Journal, over 15 million homes now have negative equity. Americans have lost about $5.3 trillion in home equity in a little over a year. Tens of millions of homeowners now found themselves with little or no equity and, in many cases, upside down on their mortgages. The once American dream has now become a nightmare. Many sleepless Americans are spinning their heads with shocking thoughts, like: "Is this the last night we will be sleeping in this home?" or "Should we just walk away from our house?" If you still have your home today and you are having problem making your payments, I urge you not to panic and let us go through all the available options that may save your home. The good news is, from a loan modification or short sale point of view, the lesser the equity, the better your chance of getting your lender to approve a modification or a short sale!

Does Home Equity Affect a Loan Modification?

One of my clients told me he recently lost his job and was having difficulty making his mortgage payment. He approached his lender for help and requested them to modify his loan to get a payment reduction. He told his lender he has been a terrific customer for many years, always paid on time, maintains a credit score of over 720, and has built up over $300,000 in home equity. As one of the "best customers", he thought his lender would bend over their back to help him before helping others. Can you sense anything wrong here? Perhaps he is an AIG executive who has no clue how the real world works! No doubt this guy will get a VIP treatment; he will be placed in front of the line for foreclosure! Think about this for a moment, if the bank knows this borrower has over $300,000 equity in the house, why would they not proceed with the foreclosure? The lender knows if they foreclose, they will be able to recover not only 100 percent of the outstanding loan balance, but possibly also any late fees, legal fees, interest or whatever they feel like adding on, to the extent permitted by law! Why would the bank even consider reducing principal or interest on an account which they have zero chance of losing money? Lenders are in the business of making money off loans. In times like this when they are losing lots of money, their goal is to minimize their losses. They are willing to modify loans to keep certain customers only if they think they will lose more money by foreclosing on their houses. Therefore, the loans that are upside down will get their top priority attention while others will become a low priority.

Chapter 10: BPO and Mini-Appraisal

When a borrower applies for a regular mortgage loan or refinancing, the lender typically orders a full appraisal by a licensed real estate appraiser of their choice. The cost of a typical appraisal of a home ranges from $350 to $500, payable by the borrower in most cases.

What is a BPO?

In the case of a loan modification or short sale, lenders typically order a BPO (Broker's Price Opinion), which is like a mini appraisal prepared by a licensed real estate broker. A regular BPO typically provides three to five comparables sales in your immediate area within the past six months. Those sales prices are then adjusted to make them as closely match as possible to your property in terms of size, age and other considerations. This can be obtained in a few days from a licensed real estate broker at a cost typically ranging from $150 to $250. Many lenders are now willing to absorb this cost on a loan modification and a short sale situation.

Some lenders would order an interior BPO, which is like a mini appraisal except it is prepared by a licensed real estate broker instead of an appraiser. In addition to a regular BPO, an interior BPO will also show pictures inside the home to determine the general condition of the home which could significantly affect the market value of the home. Most troubled borrowers have little or no money to maintain the house so the condition inside the house may be so poor that very few buyers will pay "market" price to buy the house. If they are on the verge of losing the house to foreclosure, they have no incentive to make any repairs to the house. Also, vacant homes are highly vulnerable to vandalism and the house could be torn apart. This deteriorated condition can only be reflected by a full appraisal or an interior BPO. If your house is in a poor condition, it may be to your advantage to order an interior BPO prior to submitting any request to your lender for loan modification or short sales. Otherwise, your lender may order a regular BPO from a broker outside your city and end up with a higher market value on your home than it is really worth. A BPO reflecting the low end of the valuation range will help you most on a loan modification or short sale. In today's depressed market, the low end of the value may turn out to be more accurate. Some BPOs include a neighborhood map showing where the foreclosure sales or foreclosure postings are around your home which could adversely affect the value of your home. This additional neighborhood information may be helpful in determining the true market value of your home. Normally, appraisers do not use foreclosure sales for comparables. However, this is not normal times. Foreclosure sales now dominating 30 percent to 50 percent of all sales in many market areas and they are now becoming possibly more reliable indicator of your current market value. Ignoring these foreclosure sales, on the other hand, could result in a distorted high value that neither you nor the lender is able to bring at a sale.

Can BPO Value be Manipulated?

Keep in mind that an appraisal or a BPO is not an exact science. The outcome (appraised value) can be somewhat manipulated or tilted one way or another yet still in full compliance with the laws governing real estate appraisals. To some degree, the value determined by an appraiser, or a broker in terms of a BPO, is quite subjective. For instance, if there are twenty home sales found in your area within the past six months, the average of the five highest sales (after adjusted to the equivalent of your home specifications) can be significantly higher than the average of the five lowest sales. Both are acceptable under the guidelines governing real estate appraisals, although taking the median or the average of the middle five sales may be more "accurate". For the purpose of negotiating a loan modification or short sale, it is to your benefit using the lower end of the acceptable range as the current market value. In the case of a new loan or a refinancing, lenders sometimes order a second appraisal from another appraiser just to safeguard against one appraiser leaning on one side or another of the range. This practice is particularly popular now since there was an abundance of loan frauds assisted by appraisers participated in loan scams. Lenders have just released the new Home Valuation Code of Conduct on May 1, 2009, which applies far more strict guidelines on new Fannie Mae and Freddie Mac loans. Among the guidelines are restricting to use only appraisers selected by the lenders, and licensed in the state of the property being appraised. If possible, two of the comparable sales must be within the past ninety days. Such new guidelines will help reduce future bad loans but it could also ruin sales if the appraisals are overly conservative with values far lower than the current fair market value. If lenders apply the same valuation approach on loan modifications, it is great news to those existing borrowers needing help. Although lenders typically do not base their decision on a BPO ordered by the borrower, it will still be helpful if you order one from your broker. Knowing the current market value of your home will help you determine whether you will qualify for loan modification, refinancing, short sale or other alternatives. You will be able to demonstrate to your lender how they will be better off help you with a loan modification than to foreclose, thus providing them a quick “preview” of what your situation. It may short cut you past the gate-keeper and into the hands of a loss mitigation negotiator sooner. If your BPO shows the condition of the house interior in poor condition, your lender may be convinced that your interior BPO may be more accurate than the one they ordered from a broker not in your area. Keep in mind you are probably dealing with a loss mitigation officer not residing in your state or city. Therefore, he or she has no idea the market condition of your neighborhood. They rely solely on the BPO to determine your loan-to-value ratio (see chapter 11).

Chapter 11: Loan-to-Value Ratio

Once you have determined the current market value of your home from a BPO, please calculate your Loan-to-Value Ratio (LTV) by dividing your loan balance over the current market value. If you do not want to pay your broker to get a BPO, then obtain a preliminary estimate of your home value at www.zillow.com. The estimated market value at zillow.com is not as accurate as a full BPO but it will give you some indication of what you home may be worth today. For s small fee, you may also get an estimate of your home value from www.RealQuest.com. Once you have determined your LTV, you can determine what options will suit you the best.

Does LTV Ratios Dictate Your Choice of Solutions?

The best chance to get a loan modification approved by your lender is if your LTV is between 80 percent and 130 percent. Generally speaking, Lenders set aside about 7 percent allowance for selling costs, and another 8 percent allowance for property taxes, marketing costs, etc.

if they end up foreclosing on your house. In addition, first lien lenders typically reduce the BPO value by another 10 percent for "distress sale discount" to set aside some allowance for repairs, vandalism, and maintenance. When people walked away from their house before a foreclosure, the house usually needs a lot of repairs. Empty houses, particularly those with a "foreclosure" sign in front, are prime targets for vandalism. Lenders typically choose to reduce the price instead of repairing the house. A second lien lender would discounts the BPO by 25 percent or more because they know they have very little chance of recovering their loan. Therefore, most lenders expect to net between 75 percent to 80 percent (78 percent average) of the BPO value, depends on the condition and location of the home, from selling REOs (Real Estate Owned after foreclosure). This means if your loan balance is about 78 percent of the current market value, your lender will likely recover the full loan balance from a foreclosure. Anything above 78 percent LTV means your lender will probably not recover the full amount of the loan if they foreclose on your home. Therefore, they may be better off negotiate a loan modification with you and keep your loan. The higher the LTV, the better terms you can negotiate. For example, if the market value of your home is $340,000, your lender is expecting to net about $265,200 (78 percent of $340,000) from a foreclosure. If your LTV ratio is 78 percent, then your loan balance is also $265,200. Therefore, your lender is expecting to recover 100 percent of the loan balance from the foreclosure. On the other hand, if your loan balance is $340,000, the same as your current market value (100 percent LTV), then your lender will lose $74,800 in a foreclosure. They will be better off to offer you reduced payments which they will lose less money.

If your LTV is below 70 percent, your lender will probably not be interested in any loan modification because they will be quite certain they will not lose money through foreclosure.

On the other side of the coin, if your loan-to-value ratio is over 140 percent, it will be very difficult for you to ever come out ahead. Your best bet is going to be negotiating a short sale (see chapter 21), or Deed in Lieu of Foreclosure (see chapter 26).

If your LTV falls along the border line of 70 percent to 80 percent, then you should explore the following to see if the true market value may be slightly lower, which will move the LTV ratio slightly higher:

1. Is the interior of your home in a poor condition that may lower the market value determined by lender's BPO? If so, then you should order an interior BPO with pictures to show your lender a lower market value, thus raising your LTV.
2. Is your neighborhood dominated by foreclosure sales (distressed area) or having lots of homes for sale? If so, that may bring your home value down a little further because it will probably take much longer time to sell your home (and cost your lender more money to dispose your house if foreclosed).
3. Wait a little longer and ask your broker to monitor the sales activities in your neighborhood closely to see if there are any new low sales that may help pull down your market value. If so, then order a new BPO to help you.

In conclusion, if you can convince your lender that they will lose more money if they foreclose on your home as compared to a reduced payment proposed by you, then you are already half way in the door and your chance of success is great. Please review chapter 5 Present Value Test to see how your lender determines whether to negotiate with you a loan modification. As a rule of thumb, do not expect your lender's processor to have any sympathy of your hardship situation and spend a lot of his/her time to help you. The key to a successful loan modification is the bottom line figure. You need to know what are the minimum requirements from your lender and give them what they want; it's as simple as that. If you make their jobs easier and you are qualified, the loss mitigation negotiator will be glad to help you get what you wanted, within reason.

A Quick Reference Guide Based on Various LTV Brackets

Here is a quick reference guide (general reference only, not a fixed rule):

1. Loan-to-Value Ratio is under 70 percent

If your loan balance divided by your current market value (based on the BPO) is 70 percent or below, your best solutions are:

(a) Sell your home (if necessary, increase the chance of selling by reducing your price), or lease out your home to cover your mortgage payment (see chapter 12).

(b) Refinancing (see chapter 12): Traditional (combined principal, interest, taxes and insurance (PITI) not to exceed 28 percent of gross income)

(c) Home Equity Loan (see chapter 12)

(d) Reverse Mortgage: You must be 62 years old or over (see chapter 24).

2. Loan-to-Value Ratio 70 percent to 140 percent

If your loan balance divided by your current market value (BPO) is 70 percent to 140 percent, your best solutions are one or more of the following:

(a) Loan Modification (see chapter 5): Direct through your lender. Must present:

(i) Hardship letter (see chapter 14)

(ii) A budget showing surplus after payment modified (see chapter 15)

(b) Home Affordable Loan Modification program: Must present:

(i) Hardship letter (see chapter 14)

(ii) Modified PITI not to exceed 31 percent of gross income

(c) Home Affordable Refinancing Program (see chapter 13): Key requirements are:

(i) LTV not to exceed 105 percent

(ii) Must be Fannie Mae or Freddie Mac loans

(iii) PITI not to exceed 31 percent of gross income.

(d) Forbearance – skipping or deferring some payments (see chapter 5)

(e) Debt Settlement (see chapter 20) – credit card debt relief

(f) Forensic Loan doc audit (see chapter 25) – depends on your loan documents

3. Loan-to-Value Ratio over 140 percent

If your loan balance divided by your current market value (BPO) is over 140 percent, your best solutions are:

(a) Short Sale (see chapter 21): Sell for less than loan balance

(b) Foreclosure Alternative Program (see chapter 13): Government's Short Sale program

(c) Short Refinancing (see chapter 21): Some principal forgiven in a refinancing

(d) Deed-in-Lieu of Foreclosure (see chapter 26): Deed home to your lender

(e) Forensic Loan Doc Audit (see chapter 25): Depends on loan documents

If none of these works, then you may have no alternatives other than:

(f) Foreclosure (see chapter 27): Walk away

(g) Bankruptcy (see chapter 29)

Chapter 12: Refinancing or Home Equity Loan

For those lucky ones who still have 30 percent or more equity in your home, congratulations are in order. You are in a far better shape than most Americans. However, if you are reading this book or taking our seminars, you may also be having some difficulties making your mortgage payments. Just because you have ample home equity on paper does not bring you food on the table or money to pay your mortgage, if you lost your job or encountered other forms of hardship. Your number one solution, without doubt, is to sell your house and cash out your equity. Unfortunately, in today's depressed housing market, there are far more sellers than buyers. The few buyers in the market are dominated by bargain hunters, looking for a super deal or a foreclosure. Others are mostly first time homebuyers shopping a home due to government's $8,000 tax credit incentive which will expire by the end of 2009 unless extended. In at least thirteen of the states, the state government has some programs to loan all or part of the $8,000 federal tax credit money upfront to help home buyers for down payment, and then repay the state loan later. Foreclosure sales and short sales accounted for over 30 percent of total sales in many areas. Regular sellers now found themselves lost in a sea of foreclosures; many do not receive any offer. Even when you are able to find buyers, they may not be able to find loans. To make things worse, appraisers are using low end of the range for valuations which may kill a sale. If you are not able to sell your home, and you are having problem making your mortgage payment, you may want to consider leasing your home. Hopefully, you can lease it for a monthly rent which is higher than your mortgage payment. Then you can in turn rent a cheaper dwelling unit to survive the hard times. Since a lot of would be buyers are unable to obtain a loan to buy a home, the leasing or lease/purchase option becomes very popular.

If your loan-to-value ratio is 70 percent or below, your chance of getting your loan modified is slim to none. You can always try submitting your modification request but your best options, other than selling or leasing out your home, are refinancing or getting a home equity loan.

What are the Qualifications for Refinancing?

Refinancing is completely different from a loan modification. It involves a lender taking out a new loan to replace your existing loan. Even if you get the refinancing through the same lender, your new loan will probably be owned by a different investor. Your lender may be nothing more than a loan originating or servicing entity. Once you are able to refinance your loan, your loan payment will be reduced because:

1. Current interest rate is likely to be lower than your original loan;

2. Your new loan amount should be lower than your original loan because it is based on the unpaid balance of your current loan,
3. Your new loan will probably start a new thirty year or even a forty year amortization, thus spreading out your payment over more years.

The biggest obstacle, perhaps, is that if you are suffering some kinds of hardship, chances are you may not qualify for a refinancing or a home equity loan. Qualifications for a refinancing are almost the same as applying a new loan. Typically, most lenders require that your monthly PITI (principal, interest, taxes and insurance) payment do not exceed 28 percent of your monthly gross income. For example, to refinance a $250,000 loan at 4.75 percent interest on a thirty year fixed amortization will require a monthly payment (principal & interest) of $1,305, plus an estimated property taxes and insurance of $725 a month. Total monthly PITI will be approximately $2,030. Based on the standard 28 percent qualification rule, your household income must exceed $7,250 per month or $87,000 per year to qualify.

In addition to the 28 percent rule, or the relaxed 31 percent rule under Obama's Home Affordable Refinancing program (see chapter 13), your combined total monthly debt payments, including home loans, car loans, installment loans, credit cards and other loan payments cannot exceed 36 percent of your gross income. For those who can qualify under the refinancing rules, the good news is that your lender is now willing to do it at no cost to you. However, watch out some lenders or brokers may offer you no upfront costs but they add their fees onto your loan balance so eventually you will be paying for it. They often misled you to believe that there are no fees to do a refinancing. This is almost impossible unless the broker and the new lender both are working for free. Ask to review a Good Faith Estimate (GFE) before you sign or agree to anything. Nine out of ten times they are charging you the fees by adding onto the loan balance that you are trying to refinance. If you do not know how to read a GFE, ask a Realtor friend or someone works for a title company to help you.

What is Home Equity Loan or Home Equity Line-of-Credit?

Home equity loan or home equity line-of-credit (HELOC) are completely different types of loans from refinancing. In this case, you keep your existing mortgage loan. A lender will give you a second lien mortgage loan which you can use for home improvement or debt consolidation. Such loans typically are short term loans and at higher interest rates because at a second lien position, their loan is far more risky than a first lien mortgage.

Finally, the availability of loans is a major concern. As we mentioned earlier, the secondary market typically buying mortgage loans from lenders have all but completely dried up. For the few lenders who are still providing limited home loans, their qualifications are extremely tight and their income verifications are harder than ever. Until the credit market is loosed up, most lenders will require most if not all of the following:

1. A creditor score of at least 700 (preferable 720 & above)
2. A loan-to-value ratio not to exceed 90 percent (preferable 80 percent)
3. PITI not to exceed 28 percent of gross monthly income
4. Tax returns of at least past two years
5. Financial statements listing all debts
6. Cash Flow statement
7. On a job for at least two years, W-2 form and pay stubs.
8. Bank statement for at least three months

9. Other income must be supported by verifiable documents

10. No bankruptcy listed on your credit report

Therefore, if you are looking into refinancing, try stay with the same lender who is already holding your home mortgage. You will have a much better chance of getting their approval since they have your entire payment history, and there is a chance you will be paying lower or no fees.

Refinancing generally does not affect your credit score since it is simply a rewritten mortgage. If you are qualified to refinance, this is a good time to do it since fixed interest rates are unlikely to go back below 5 percent.

Chapter 13: Making Home Affordable Programs

In October 2007 when the first sign of a serious problem forthcoming, a program named Hope Now was created to help homeowners.

What is Hope Now Program?

Hope Now is a private sector alliance among HUD approved counseling agents, mortgage servicing companies, investors and other mortgage market participants, that provides free foreclosure prevention assistance to homeowners. This program, originally aimed at saving 400,000 homeowners, has been mostly a dismal success with very few troubled homeowners qualified. This program is only open to member companies who chose to join the alliance and, as of April 2009, there are only twenty-six mortgage servicing companies joined. The program is focusing on refinancing serious delinquent loans at lower rates and credit counseling. Unfortunately, most troubled homeowners do not qualify under this program. The result so far has been mostly disappointed.

The Homeownership Preservation Foundation, a Hope Now member, created and operates the Homeowners HOPE Hotline (1-888-995-HOPE). There is no cost to homeowners for contacting a nonprofit counselor by calling the Hotline number.

In April 2009, Hope Now initiated their "Reach Out" campaign on a targeted state-by-state basis, sending out letters to homeowners in states with the highest percentage of extremely delinquent borrowers, including Wisconsin, New Jersey, Texas, South Carolina and Florida.

In late 2008, the Obama Administration unveiled a $75 billion foreclosure relief plan to help troubled homeowners called *"Making Home Affordable"* Programs. These programs reach out to far more homeowners than the private Hope Now program. Through these "Making Home Affordable" Programs, as many as nine million American families may be eligible to refinance or modify their loans to reduced payments that are affordable. There are still a lot of restrictions, though. For most troubled homeowners, they will still have a better chance dealing directly with their lenders on either refinancing or loan modification.

Are You Qualified for Home Affordable Refinancing?

The first part of the program is the Home Affordable Refinance Program. To qualify:

1. You must be the owner-occupant of a one to four unit home;
2. Loans must be owned or securitized by Fannie Mae or Freddie Mac;

3. You must be current (not more than thirty day late in the past 12 months) on your loan payment, cannot be delinquent;
4. You must have income and be able to make the new payment if refinancing is approved;
5. Loan-to-value ratio not to exceed 105 percent, based on current market value of your home at the time you apply;
6. PITI cannot exceed 31 percent of your gross income;

There is no closing cost if you are qualified under this program. Basically, this program is targeted to creditworthy homeowners who have been unable to take advantage of today's lower interest rates through traditional refinancing because their homes have decreased in value. As we discussed in chapter 11, in a traditional refinancing, most lenders requires the loan-to-value ratio between 75 percent to 90 percent, but under this Making Home Affordable Program, the LTV can be as high as 105 percent for the first lien mortgage lender. If there is a second lien holder, they will have to agree to stay on the second position. Also, the PITI can be as high as 31 percent of your gross income instead of the traditional 28 percent. Based on our earlier example in chapter 11, the new 31 percent rule will drop the household income requirement from $7,250 per month to $6,548 per month, or from $87,000 per year to $78,580 per year. Interest rate under this program will be based on market rates in effect at the time of the refinance, and any associated points and fees quoted by the lender. This program will not reduce the principal amount owed.

Since the government nationalized Fannie Mae and Freddie Mac, this program is aimed at helping loans owned by the government. Those truly troubled homeowners who are behind in their payments or are upside down on their loan-to-value ratio will be left behind. Those homeowners will have to rely on loan modifications. Since payment must be current to qualify under this program, a lot of troubled homeowners will not be qualified. While it is doubtful if the government can help as many as nine million borrowers they intended, it is still considered in the industry a far better program than the private Hope Now program. This program will expire on June 10, 2010 unless extended. To find out whether your loan is owned by Fannie Mae or Freddie Mac, you can call 1-800-7Fannie, visit www.fanniemae.com/loanlookup, www.freddiemac.com/mymortgage or call 1-800-Freddie

Are you qualified for Home Affordable Loan Modification ?

The second part of the program is Home Affordable Modification Program. This program will help borrowers who are already behind on their payments but are unable to continue making the existing mortgage payment due to a hardship situation. The government will provide mortgage servicers with financial incentives such as $1,000 per year per loan subsidy and reducing interest rate to as low as 2 percent, to help modify existing first lien mortgages. The government hopes to help as many as three to four million homeowners avoid foreclosure regardless of who owns or services the mortgage. To qualify:

1. You must be owner-occupant of a one to four unit home
2. Unpaid principal balance not to exceed $729,750 for one unit home (higher limit for two to four unit properties)
3. Loan originated on or before January 1, 2009
4. Your existing mortgage payment is more than 31 percent of your gross monthly income
5. You cannot afford to make existing payment due to hardship situation.

Not all loan servicers participate in this program. Participation is strictly voluntary. Due to the financial incentives, however, most major lenders are expected to participate. The primary goal is to modify your first lien mortgage payments so that the new payment will fall below 31 percent of your gross monthly income. All past due charges (interest, taxes, insurance and costs that your lender paid to other parties on your behalf will be added to the loan balance but you will not have to pay any loan modification fee or pay any past due late fees which will be waived. If dropping interest rate down to 2 percent will still not make your payment fall below 31 percent, then the lenders may consider extending your payment term to lower the payment further. If that still does not work, the lenders, at their sole option, may defer repayment on a portion of the amount you owe until a later time. This is called a principal forbearance. Such amount will be treated more like a separate interest free loan with a balloon payment so your regular mortgage payment will fall below the 31 percent threshold. The lenders, at their sole discretion, may choose to forgive this amount later to make it work.

As I discussed previously under regular loan modification (see chapter 5) and LTV (see chapter 11), your LTV is a key indicator whether your lender will consider you under this program. If you have too much equity (LTV below 75 percent), the lender will probably reject your loan modification because the investor behind the loan will be better off to foreclose. Under this program, your lender will conduct an internal value test (based on their BPO) which simply compares the total cost of loan modification (i.e. lender's concession resulted from reduced payments) versus how much they may lose in a foreclosure. The bottom line is whether the lender (or its investors) will be better off approving your loan modification. As long as you fully understand that all loan modifications, whether they are under the government programs or directly through your lender, must end up in a win-win situation for both you and your lender.

If approved, you will actually be placed on a trial period of three months at the new interest rate (below market rate) and reduced payment level. If you successfully make the payments and are current at the end of the trial period, your servicer will enter into a permanent modification agreement that will lower your interest rate to a fixed rate for five years, and then capped at a low rate for the remaining life of the loan. Maximum interest rate increase after five years is 1 percent, not to exceed the pre-agreed cap rate. Property taxes and insurance will be escrowed each month even if your original loan does not require such escrow.

When you apply for a Home Affordable Modification, your loan servicer will analyze your monthly debts, including the amount you will owe on the new mortgage payment after it is modified, as well as payments on as second mortgage, car loans, credit cards or child support. If the sum of all of these recurring monthly expenses is equal to or more than 55 percent of your gross monthly income, you must agree to participate in housing counseling provided by a HUD-approved housing counselor as a condition of getting the modification.

Borrowers who make timely payments on their modified loans will be rewarded with bonus incentives. For every month you make a payment on time, the government will pay an incentive that reduces the principal balance on your loan. The incentives, up to $1,000 per year, will be applied directly to your loan balance annually and over five years. The total principal reduction could add up to $5,000. This contribution by the government will help you build equity faster.

This program, which opens to non-Fannie Mae or Freddie Mac loans and homeowners already behind in their payments, is far more aggressive and helpful than any other programs introduced by the government so far. It is expected to help millions of troubled homeowners. However, under this program, PITI based on the modified payment cannot exceed 31 percent of your gross monthly income. In comparison, the typical loan modification direct from your lender only requires to show a positive cash flow with PITI generally not exceeding 50 percent of your gross income. Therefore, those homeowners in deeper trouble in terms of cash flow may have to resort to the typical loan modification not under this government program.

Foreclosure Alternative Program

This is the latest of Obama Administration's programs, setting incentives and uniform procedures for short sales (see chapter 21) under its Foreclosure Alternative Program (FAP). It is targeted to borrowers who are unable to retain their homes under the Making Home Affordable Loan Modification Program. Under this program, the lender may consider a short sale or, if that is not successful, a deed-in-lieu of foreclosure (see chapter 26). Here are some of the preliminary guidelines:

1. Borrowers/Homeowners: Borrowers/homeowners qualify under the FAP if they meet minimum eligibility requirements for the Home Affordable Modification program but are unable to retain their home under the program. Before proceeding with a foreclosure, lenders must determine if a short sale is appropriate.
2. Incentives - Incentives include: (a) $1,000 to lenders or servicers for successful completion of a short sale or deed-in-lieu of foreclosure; (b) $1,500 for borrowers/ homeowners to help with relocation expenses; and (c) up to $1,000 toward the cost of paying junior mortgage or lien holders to release their liens

(one dollar from the government for every two dollars paid by the investors to the second lien holders).

3. Standardized Documents: The program will include streamlined and standardized documents, including a Short Sale Agreement and an Offer Acceptance Letter. The goal is to minimize complexity and increase use of the short sale option.

4. Property Valuation by Appraisal or BPO (see chapter 10): Lenderss will independently establish both property value and minimum acceptable net return, in accordance with investor requirements. The price may be determined based on an appraisal or one or more broker price opinions (BPO), issued no more than 120 days before the date of the short sale agreement.

5. Time Line: In the Short Sale Agreement, lenders must give borrowers/ homeowners at least 90 days to market and sell the property, or up to one year, depending on market conditions. Property must be listed with a licensed real estate professional with experience in the neighborhood. No foreclosure may take place during the marketing period (at least 90 days) specified in the Short Sale Agreement.

6. Sales Expenses: The Short Sale Agreement must specify the reasonable and customary real estate commissions and costs that may be deducted from the sales price. The lender must agree not to negotiate a lower commission after an offer has been received.

7. No Borrower Fees: Lenders may not charge fees to borrower/ homeowners for participating in the FAP.

8. Program Expiration: The program is in effect through 2012

9. Deed-in-Lieu of Foreclosure Option: Lenders have the option to require the borrower/homeowner to agree to deed the

property to the lender in exchange for a release from the debt if the property does not sell within the time allowed in the Short Sale Agreement.

Chapter 14: Hardship Letter - Loan Modification

All lenders require a hardship letter for either loan modification or short sale. The common myth of a hardship letter is that your lender wants you to tell them a long sad story and begging them for sympathy. This is not a "sad story" competition to decide who has the "worst" hardship so you will be rewarded with a payment reduction! The most important part of the hardship letter is not the reason of the hardship but the solution. Although no one will admit it openly, the loss mitigation negotiator does not really care about your hardship reasons; he just need a valid reason so he can put a check mark on the list. Remember, everyone he is dealing with everyday is supposed to be in some kind of hardship situation. Having said that, you will still need to state a valid and truthful hardship reason, because they will read your hardship letter. Your lender may verify your bank statement to see if your deposits or income dropped after you suffered a hardship. This is because the lenders do not want to grant you concessions if you lied to them about a hardship. Some borrowers are seeking for a lower payment even if they can afford the current payments. In any case, most lenders prefer you keep the hardship explanation simple and skip the long story.

List of Acceptable Hardship Reasons

Here are some typical valid hardship reasons acceptable to your lender:

1. Lost of job (you or a co-borrower)
2. Job relocation
3. Divorce or Separation
4. Natural disaster or other casualty losses
5. Auto accident or other injuries
6. Surgery or other medical reasons
7. Military duty
8. ARM loan reset, unable to refinance
9. Reduced income
10. Business failure
11. Increased expenses beyond your control
12. Children going to college
13. A lawsuit or a judgment against you
14. Death to a co-borrower (but not all borrowers) because your lender cannot deal with a loan when none of the borrowers is still alive.

Be accurate on the approximate time the hardship occurred because when your lender verifies your bank statements and credit card statements, they can find out when your income reduced or expenses increased.

What Lenders Looking for in Your Hardship Letter?

Once you get through with your hardship reason, then the most important part of the hardship letter your lender wants to know if what are you doing to resolve your hardship situation and whether you will be able to survive if they do help you reduce your payments. While most people know they need to provide a hardship letter, few people know what the lenders really want to see in a hardship letter. People get rejected by their lenders because they failed to describe what they are doing or planning to do to get out of the hardship situation. The solutions you proposed in your letter must coincide with the proposed budget and cash flow (see chapter 15). The three basic components of a hardship letter are:

1. What got you into a mess;
2. Where you are now; and
3. How you are going to get out of this mess.

The key is to reassure the lender that your hardship is over or coming to an end. Explain what you intend to do in order to balance your proposed budget. This will tie in with what concessions you are asking your lender to give you. You must demonstrate to your lender that you are willing to make a lot of sacrifices, along with negotiating with other parties (such as second mortgage holder, credit card lenders) if appropriate, and that they are your last resort to make your budget work.

Sample Hardship Letter #1

Date

Your names

Address

Loss Mitigation Department

Lender Name

Address

Re: Loan Modification Request on Loan # ________

To Whom It May Concern:

I am writing this letter to explain our unfortunate set of circumstances that have caused us to become delinquent on our mortgage. (Insert hardship reason here and keep it short and straight forward). We have done everything in our power to make ends meet but unfortunately we have fallen short and would like you to consider working with us to modify our loan. Our number one goal is to keep our home and we would really appreciate the opportunity to do that. It is our full intention to pay our debts but, at this time, we have exhausted all our savings, and we are turning to you for help.

(Insert the approximate time of hardship occurred, and whether it is temporary or permanent)

Our situation has gotten better because (insert reasons here). Unfortunately, as much as we tried to cut our budget down to bare necessities and maximize our income resources, we are still a bit short of balancing our budget. As shown in the proposed budget enclosed, if (your bank's name) is willing to modify the payment down by $________

a month, we will be able to continue making new mortgage payments and avoid losing our home. We believe such a loan modification will benefit both parties. Therefore, we sincerely request that our loan be modified as follows:

Reduce interest rate from ______% to ______%;

Re-amortize the loan balance plus missing payments over ________ years; and Waive any late fees incurred so far;

Such modification will reduce the monthly mortgage payment from $_________ to $________, thus enable us to balance out budget.

We truly hope that you will consider working with us and we are anxious to get this matter resolved.

Sincerely,

Borrower's signature

Co-borrower's signature

Enclosures

Sample Hardship Letter #2

Date

Your names

Address

Loss Mitigation Department

Lender Name

Address

Re: Loan Modification Request for Loan # ________

To Whom It May Concern:

Due to the recent rate adjustment to the mortgage we currently have with your company, we are having great difficulties to afford the new payment. We have a five year fixed rate which is now adjustable and is scheduled to adjust again in November 2009. Considering our income, there will be no way we can afford the increased payments come November. It appears the only way to avoid default and help stop foreclosure on our home is to modify our loan.

Is it possible to have our current adjustable rate mortgage converted to a fixed rate? Alternatively, can you suggest other ways to modify our loan to prevent payments going up so we can keep our home? We have considered refinancing but apparently, there is a significant drop in our home value in the past two years which prevented us from any refinancing possibilities. If you can somehow hold the payment without increase for the next 36 months, perhaps we will be able to refinance by then.

Based on the BPO and an analysis by my real estate broker, my home has a current fair market value of $340,000, while my loan balance is $343,700. If you foreclose on my home, the likely amount you will net from a REO sale will be around $266,000. I do not assume to be able to dictate your calculations, but I estimated the present value of the loan, if modified per my request, will net your bank about $311,275 present value. It appears there is no doubt we both will benefit from this proposed loan modification. Time is of essence. I want to thank you in advance for your time and consideration.

Sincerely,

Borrower's signature

Co-Borrower's signature

Enclosures

Chapter 15 Budget & Cash Flow

The single most important element of a loan modification package is your budget and cash flow. It must meet your lenders requirements or you will be rejected. In addition, all income and expense figures must be verifiable and supported by documents. Your lenders may request to see your bank statement, credit card statements, utilities bills, etc. to verify your figures. Lenders are savvy enough to know the average cost of utilities, groceries, car insurance, etc. For example, on groceries, lenders typically use a nationwide average of $150 per adult per month, and $75 to $125 per child per month. Therefore, if you put $200 groceries a month for a family of four, they know you are not telling the truth. Also, do not think you can hide some credit card statements. Your credit report will show every one of your active credit cards, the current balances, and the minimum monthly payments. Remember, lenders can only verify you past expenses which obviously end with a deficit or you do not need to ask for help. The most important thing your lenders want to see is your proposed budget. As long as your proposed budget showed reasonable figures, and you end with a surplus once they modified your payments, you will meet their requirements.

No matter how hard it may seem, you can usually fit your budget to the lenders expectations by removing non-essentials from the budget, unless there is a very large deficit. Even so, you should be able to dig deep enough and find ways to explain and ways to overcome it. The budget goes hand-in-hand with your hardship explanation and your proposed solutions.

Some Basic Rules to Follow:

Here are some of the basic rules to follow:

1. As far as your lender is concern, your household income was sufficient to meet your normal budget, including making existing mortgage payment, before you encountered your hardship.
2. Due to the sudden hardship (see chapter 14), either your income suddenly reduced or your expenses suddenly go up drastically. As a result, you are unable to continue making your mortgage payment. You need to prepare a current budget showing all your income and expenses and show a deficit at the bottom to demonstrate you need help to balance your budget. These figures must be supported by bank statements, credit card statements, W-2 forms and pay stubs. If you do not show a deficit, then you should be able to make the mortgage payment without needing help from your bank.
3. In order to avoid a foreclosure, you are requesting your lender to reduce your loan payment to help you balance your budget.
4. Your lender will not want to be the only one making concessions and sacrifices. First, they want you to demonstrate what you are planning to do on order to balance your budget.. Then,

they want to see other creditors also participate in offering concessions to help you balance your budget. This is particularly important when you are dealing with the first lien mortgage lender and you are also paying a second lien mortgage which has the most risk if you walk away.

5. Next, you will need to prepare a new budget to show each lender what you are asking them to do for a loan modification. In this new proposed budget, you need to list all the expenses you plan to trim and, show the reduced mortgage payments from each lender if they agree to what modification you proposed. The bottom line figure of this proposed monthly budget must show a surplus figure. Most lenders like to see a surplus figure ranges from $250 to $500, but some require a higher surplus. Please review chapter 18 to see some guidelines set by major lenders. If the bottom figure is still a deficit number, almost all lenders will reject your application. This is because if you are unable to pay the reduced loan payment per your request, why should they even border to modify your loan? If they believe they will have to foreclose later, then they would rather foreclose now and save all the troubles. Therefore, if your new figure is still showing a deficit, go back and look for more areas to trim your expenses or find a way to increase your income before submitting the loan modification package! Obviously, you do not want to end up with a surplus figure too high that they believe you do not need their help.

In your new proposed budget, the total amount of PITI (principal, interest, taxes and insurance) should not be more than 50 percent of your gross monthly income if you are submitting loan modification request directly to your lender. Under the Obama's Home Affordable Modification program (see chapter 13), however, the proposed PITI must be below 31 percent of the monthly gross income.

Make sure you keep all your supporting documents organized and be ready to present to the lender. Some lenders would prefer to go through your budget on the phone to pre-qualify you before accepting your application for a loan modification.

Case Study

Let us review the following Case Study: Mr. & Mrs. Smith bought a $300,000 home in Texas five years ago. They paid $15,000 (5 percent down) and financed $285,000 (95 percent) with a first lien mortgage of $280,000 (80 percent) at 7 percent interest and a second lien mortgage at 9 percent interest. Mr. Smith has a consulting job, making about $67,000 a year. Mrs. Smith is an administrative assistant, making about $45,000 a year. They have a thirteen year old daughter *Kimberly* enrolled in a private school. They have two cars, with one car payment remaining, and they take a couple of vacations a year. They are a devoted Christian family living a comfortable life. However, like most young American families, they do not have much money in savings. Then all of a sudden, Mrs. Smith lost her job. Despite trying hard, she could not land another job in this market. So she is collecting unemployment benefits, but they are still running at a deficit of about $1,800 a month. Soon, their small savings are depleted and they are unable to continue making mortgage payments. They do not want to lose their home so they want to negotiate with their lenders to reduce the payments to avoid foreclosure. Now comes the hard part, where are they going to cut their expenses? Who's going to take the most sacrifices, Mr. Smith, Mrs. Smith, or Kimberly? They ran the budget about twenty times and still end up with a deficit. No one wants to give up his/her favorite things, whether it's a premium cable channel, an annual ski trip, donations to church, a Blackberry phone, or transferring to a public school. At the end, in order to save their home, the family decided everyone has to sacrifice in order to survive. Hence, they managed to trim down their deficit significantly. Here are sacrifices they are proposing to do:

1. Cutting their utilities bills from $350 to $325 by turning temperatures higher and using more fans in the house.
2. Cutting out their home phone and switching the Blackberry to a regular cell phone with lower minutes so their phone bills will be reduced from $135 to $55.
3. Cutting out the cable TV premium channels and downgrading the Internet packages which will enable them to trim the bills from $120 to $65 per month.
4. Kimberly's allowance will be cut from $75 to $50 a month and transferring her from the private school to a public school will save another $450 a month (This is probably the hardest item to cut as Kimberly went on a hunger strike to protest. After dad teased her for helping to cut down their food budget, she started eating again).
5. Although they have been faithfully donating $50 a week to their church, they must face a tough decision here. The Bible teaches them to sacrifice and give their wealth to God. Unfortunately, the lender is not going to agree to a payment reduction so they can donate the money to their church. So, after praying hard for forgiveness, they cut their church donations temporary, which save them $200 a month.
6. They have to share a car more often in order to save some gasoline and repair bills by $65 a month.
7. They cut down on groceries and household supplies by $50 a month by using more coupons and buy less expensive food.

8. No more vacation trips or nail salons. They are eliminating almost all leisure travel, entertainment, beauty salons, restaurant eating, and spending which will save them $375 a month.

Now that they have demonstrated all the sacrifices they are willing to do, then they will turn to lenders for help in order to balance their budget.

9. Enroll in a debt settlement program (see chapter 20) with a payment plan to trim credit card minimum payment from $495 to $295 a month.
10. They are requesting the second lien mortgage lender to modify their loan by reducing the interest rate from 9 percent to 3 percent on the $42,970 principal balance for the remaining twenty-five years of the loan. Assuming they will agree, the second mortgage payment will be reduced from $346 to $204 a month. The second lien lender is more likely to agree because in the event of a foreclosure, they may get totally wipe out by the first lien lender. If the figures still show a deficit, perhaps asking for some principal reduction from the second lien holder will help.
11. Finally, they will request the first lien mortgage lender to trim their interest rate from 7 percent down to 3 percent on the $225,916 principal balance for the remaining twenty-five years of the loan, and to waive all later fees accrued. If approved, the monthly payment will be reduced from $1,596 to $1,071 (as an alternative, they can try asking lender to extend the loan terms to a new thirty year or forty year amortization to reduce the mortgage payment).

As you can see from this Case Study, there are many ways to trim a budget. You must set your priorities and go down the list until you balance your budget. If your lender sees that your proposed budget still include non-necessity items such as shopping, leisure travel or a movie channel, they are not going to approve what you requested. In this case study, the Smith family has demonstrated they are willing to sacrifice as much as they can to keep their home. Since their LTV is around 95 percent, and the proposed budget will end with a surplus of $394, the lenders will most likely approve their loan modification request.

Aside from cutting expenses, sometimes borrowers overlooked the possibility of some extra income. Mrs. Smith may be able to find other jobs even if she cannot find another secretary job. She may find a part time tutoring job to help bring some income. Mr. Smith may have to get a second job to help out. Sometimes you need to think outside the box. What if you rent out a room above the garage?

Even if you cannot find another income source, you may be able to get a personal loan from friends and relatives. Lenders will accept monthly loan from a personal source if it can be verified with bank deposits and a letter signed by the person giving you the loan stating the amount and terms of the loan.

Mr. & Mrs. Smith	Monthly Budget and Cash Flow			
	Current		Proposed	
INCOME:	Borrower	Co-Borrower	Borrower	Co-Borrower
Gross salary/wages	$ 5,000		$ 5,000	
Overtime pay	$ 600		$ 600	
Unemployment benefits		$ 820		$ 820
Total gross income	$ 5,600	$ 820	$ 5,600	$ 820
Deductions:				
Federal Income Tax	$ (965)		$ (965)	
FICA	$ (428)		$ (428)	
Net Income	$ 4,207	$ 820	$ 4,207	$ 820
Net Income - Combined		$ 5,027		$ 5,027

EXPENSES (Combined):	Current		Proposed
Primary Home 1st lien mortgage	$ 1,596		$ 1,071
Primary Home 2nd lien mortgage	$ 346		$ 204
Taxes on primary home if not included	$ 766		$ 766
Insurance primary home if not included	$ 76		$ 76
Maintenance on homes	$ 100		$ 100
Auto loan payment - 1st car	$ 396		$ 396
Credit cards debts - minimum payments	$ 495		$ 295
Utilities electric/gas, water/sewer, garbage	$ 350		$ 325
HOA dues (monthly)	$ 50		$ 50
Telephone - home & cell	$ 135		$ 55
Cable TV & Internet	$ 120		$ 65
Child Care / Day care	$ 75		$ 50
School tuition & books	$ 500		$ 50
Vehicle - gas	$ 400		$ 350
Vehicle - maintenance, repairs & parking	$ 75		$ 60
Charity or church donations	$ 200		
Insurance – health & life	$ 50		$ 50
Insurance - vehicles	$ 175		$ 175
Medical expenses not insurance covered	$ 45		$ 45
Groceries & Toiletries	$ 450		$ 400
Shopping - clothing, etc	$ 100		$ 30
Entertainment - restaurants, movies	$ 100		
Travel - non business reimbursed	$ 75		
Spending money - other miscellaneous	$ 100		$ 20
Other expenses (specify) - salons	$ 50		

Total monthly expenses	**$ 6,825**		**$ 4,583**
Surplus or (deficit)	**$ (1,798)**		**$ 394**

Proposed budget shows PITI at 42 percent of gross income after modified. This will meet the requirement of regular loan modification but not Home Affordable Modification program.

Typical Lender's Income and Expense Budget Form

Always put all borrowers names, mailing address, contact numbers (best time to call), and your loan number(s) on top (if two loans, list both).

Lender's Borrower's Monthly Income Form

BORROWER'S MONTHLY INCOME

Borrower #1: ____________________ **LOAN#:** ________________

Borrower # 2: ____________________

	MONTHLY PAYROLL	1st PERSON	2nd PERSON	TOTAL
Gross Salary/ Wages				
Overtime pay				
Commissions				
Bonuses				
S	**Federal Income Tax**			
U	**FICA**			
B	**State Income Tax**			
T	**401 K**			
R	**Health Insurance**			
A	**Life Insurance**			
C	**Other**			

T	Other			

TOTAL PAYROLL:			

ADDITIONAL MONTHLY INCOME

	BANK ACCOUNTS	1st PERSON	2nd PERSON	TOTAL
Interest				
Dividends				
	FAMILY			
Alimony				
Child Support				
	MISCELLANEOUS			
Disability				
Retirement				
Rental Property				
	OTHER (Please List)			

ADDITIONAL INCOME:			

ADD your Total Payroll and Total Additional Income

PAYROLL:			
ADDITIONAL INCOME: +			
MONTHLY NET INCOME:			

OTHER FUNDS	1st PERSON	2nd PERSON	TOTAL
Savings Accounts			
Life Insurance			
Stocks/Bonds			

TOTAL OTHER FUNDS:			

Lender's Borrower's Monthly Expenses Form

BORROWER'S

MONTHLY EXPENSES

BORROWER 1: 1st LOAN #:

BORROWER 2: 2nd Loan #:

DESCRIPTION	MONTHLY PAYMENT	BALANCE DUE	# OF MONTHS BEHIND
HOUSE LOANS			
1st Mortgage Lender			
2nd Mortgage Lender			
OTHER LOANS			
#1			
#2			
Car 1			
Car 2			
CREDIT CARDS			
#1			
#2			
#3			
#4			
UTILITIES			
Electricity			
Gas			
Telephone			
Water/Sewer			
Cable TV			
MEDICAL EXPENSES			
Health Insurance **If you pay*			
Life Insurance **If you pay*			
Doctor/Dentist Bills			
Prescriptions			
Hospital Bills			
CAR EXPENSES			
Gasoline			
Auto Insurance			
Parking			
Maintenance			
FOOD			
Family at Home			
School Lunches			

Work Lunches			
CLOTHING			
New Clothes/Shoes			
Dry Cleaning			
ENTERTAINMENT			
Movies			
Dining Out			
Vacations			
Spending Money			
OTHER			
Church			
Clubs or Union Dues			
Sports			
Hobbies			
OTHER (Please List)			

TOTAL:			

Profit and Loss Statement

If you are self employed, your lender will require you to show a Profit and Loss Statement for at least the past six months. You can include more months if that will help bring up your average income. Any income stated must be verifiable by showing deposits on your bank statements. Here is a simple example. You can easily prepare your own if you have all the figures or your accountant can prepare one for you. Once you derive the average monthly income, you will then use that figure for your budget.

ABC Company

PROFIT and LOSS STATEMENT

For the period 1/1/09 - 6/30/09

Income:		
Gross Receipts:		**$ 67,983**
Expenses:		
Advertising / Marketing	**$ 11,236**	
Office supplies & expenses	**$ 594**	
Rent & phones	**$ 1,325**	
Payroll & Payroll taxes	**$ 18,350**	
Auto expenses	**$ 369**	
Insurance	**$ 965**	
Other expenses	**$ 454**	
TOTAL EXPENSES		**$ 33,293**
Net Income		**$ 34,690**
Average monthly income		**$ 5,782**

What Your Lender is looking for in Your Budget?

Ideally, you want to get your proposed budget to end with a surplus figure ranges from $250 to $500. This is because $250 will allow you a small reserve for any unforeseen expenses like fixing a flat tire, or insurance premium increase. If you end up over $500 surplus, then your lender will have less incentive to give you any significant concession. Please review chapter 18 to see specific guidelines of major lenders.

Budget Audit

Finally, be truthful in your budget because, if not, your lender is trained to detect your lies. Here are some tips on accounting audit:

1. Your income can be verified from your recent pay stubs, as well as last year's W-2 forms and tax returns, and converting into a monthly figure. Your lender can also cross reference to the deposits shown on your bank statements that you must provide.
2. If you list any other income, you must provide your lender proofs. For example, if you stated you will get a monthly loan from your uncle, you must provide a signed letter from your uncle and deposits shown on your bank statements.
3. Don't think your lender do not know about all your credit cards. They will order a credit report which lists all your debts. So if you try to hide some credit card debts, they will know. Your credit report will also show the minimum payment required on each of your credit card so if you put a credit card payment on

your budget that is substantially different, they will know you are not telling the truth.

4. If you elect to enroll in a debt settlement program (see chapter 20) to reduce some of your debts, you must provide your lender evidence of such enrollment and the monthly payment under that program.
5. Lenders have general information on average cost of living in your city. They have some general guideline how much it will cost a family on groceries, utilities, etc expenses. So, you cannot put in an extremely low figure thinking your lender from out of state will not know.
6. As far as other expenses like entertainment, restaurant eating, travel, shopping, etc expenses, some lenders want copies of your credit card statement to see if you are telling the truth. If they see on your credit card statement that you are charging items like country club membership fee, travel to Las Vegas, bought some new furniture, etc, they know you are not really in a hardship so they will not approve you for reduced loan payments.

Focus your time and effort on your proposed budget, either try to find new sources of income or ways to trim expenses. There is not much you can change on your current budget. It is always difficult to make sacrifices when your family is under a lot of stress. Everyone in your family has to work together to get through this difficult times. What you do not want to do is to saving the house but losing your family. Hopefully, the sacrifices are temporary.

It may be helpful to order your own credit report (it's free and do not affect your credit score. See chapter 31) so you can make sure your figures will match your report. If you conduct a self audit to make sure all documents matching what you put on the budget, it will help speed up the process and avoid rejection.

To look up your proposed mortgage payment using reduced interest rate and/or extended payment years, most mortgage lender's website has a mortgage calculator page whereby you can enter the loan amount, interest rate, number of amortization years and your monthly payment (principal and interest only) will be printed out. If you have trouble finding one, try the following calculator link to Countrywide (now acquired by Bank of America):

www.countrywide.com/calculators/calculator.
aspx?CalcType=WhatsMyPmt

You can try to play with the rates and number of amortization years to see what payment will help you reach your target budget. Once you have determined such, then you need to see if that's a reasonable modification request to your lender. In chapter 18, you can review many case studies to learn what you may reasonably expect from your lender.

Chapter 16 Lenders' Check List

Most lenders have their own check list of documents needed to process a loan modification or short sale. Please review chapter 18 for more specifics from each lender. Generally, most of the following documents will be required.

What are the Documents Required by Your Lender?

In chapter 18, specific documents required by major lenders are listed. In general, all or most of the following documents are needed by lenders:

1. Hardship letter (see chapter 14): Hardship reasons and your proposed solution
2. Budget and Cash Flow (see chapter 15): Show a positive figure after loan modified.
3. Loan modification application form and cover letter.

4. Your mortgage statements: Both lenders if more than one lender.
5. Copy of Notice of Default or Notice of Trustee Sale if issued.
6. Credit report (see chapter 31): Your lender will order this. You may want to order one yourself to help you prepare the budget to match your credit report.
7. BPO (see chapter 10): Your lender will order this to determine the LTV. It may be helpful if you order one and include in your package to help demonstrate how the lender will be better off to reduce your loan payment as proposed than to lose more money in foreclosure.
8. W-2 forms (two years), 1099 forms and most current thirty days pay stubs.
9. Overtime, bonus or commission pay: Verification of employment, year-to-date pay stubs with expense information, letter from employer itemize base pay, hours, base rate, overtime rate, bonus rate, commission for two years, average of hours worked, average bonus, etc.
10. Other proof of Income
11. Last one or two years of tax returns (all schedules).
12. Two months of most recent bank statements.
13. Property taxes statement and proof of payment if not escrowed.
14. Proof of insurance coverage and payment if not escrowed.
15. If enrolled in debt settlement program (see chapter 20), show evidences.
16. If there is rental income, copy of the lease agreement.
17. If you have Social Security income: Form SSA – 1099

18. If you have receivable income: Copy of the note and proof of interest income.
19. If you have alimony and child support income or payment: Copy of ratified agreement and/or decrees, proof of stable payments, tax forms, court records, cancelled checks and deposit records for one year.
20. For those self employed, one or two years of business tax returns, year-to-date (at least the most recent six months) profit and loss statement, and verification of ownership. If you own greater than 25 percent of a corporation or partnership, then submit two years of corporate tax returns with income statement, K-1 partnership forms.
21. Interest and Dividends: Year to date broker and bank statements
22. Future raises: Letter from your employer, giving certainty, time and amount of new rate of pay.
23. Employee benefits: Letter from employer itemizing, pay stubs.
24. Credit card statements: Some lender may ask for credit card statement of recent months to verify your expenses.

You should be prepared to have all this items ready to present to your lender. Otherwise, if you submit an incomplete package, they will kick it back to you asking you for the missing documents. It will speed up your loan modification process, and increase your chance of approval, if you are fully prepared. Besides, you will need many of these items to help you prepare your budget. Just organize all documents in one folder and make copies.

Chapter 17 VA Loan Modification

This is only available on VA loans. VA will buy the loan from your lender through a refinancing. Outstanding payments are added to the principal and the mortgage is re-amortized to lower your payments.

Who Will Qualify?

VA home loan guaranties are issued to help eligible service members, veterans, reservists and unmarried surviving spouses buy or refinance a home. To be eligible, in addition to the service requirements (a valid Certificate of Eligibility – COE), borrower must have a good credit rating, sufficient income, and the home must be a principal residence. For more information, check with the United States Department of Veterans Affairs at www.homeloans.va.gov/.

Chapter 18 What to Expect from Lenders?

As I discussed in chapter 5, loan modification will result in lower mortgage payment for the borrower with one or more of the following changes made on an existing loan:

1. Lowering the interest rate of an existing loan. Some lenders now offer step rates starting at 3 percent interest only for three years and then move up to 4 percent in year four and then fixed at 5 percent in year five and the remaining twenty years.
2. Extending the paying term over more years. More lenders are extending to forty year amortization if that's what it takes to make the payment low enough to balance your budget.
3. Converting ARM (adjustable rate mortgage) or an interest only loan to a fixed loan with lower interest. This is almost automatic if you are still holding ARM loan with more rate adjustment coming.
4. Forbearance – skipping one or more payments. Some lenders are willing to forgo a couple (usually two or three) of payments but not all lenders willing to do so.

5. Principal reduction – Only in some extreme upside down cases that lenders are willing to accept principal reduction. In most cases, however, it ends up with a short sale or deed-in-lieu of foreclosure. As an alternative, many lenders now offer a silent second mortgage at 0 percent interest which will simply push some part of principal to a side loan at 0 percent interest so that you will be able to make the modified loan payment. The silent second may be waived and written off at the option of the lender at a future date. Legally, you will still owe the side loan amount but without interest.

In many cases, lenders will agree on a conditional loan modification. They will place you on a three (or more) month trial period. If you can demonstrate you are able to make the modified payment on time, then they will finalize a permanent modification agreement with you.

There are also many lenders require you to put up a good faith payment or contribution, which is a percentage of your past due payments and fees. This number is sometimes negotiable and sometimes not. For example, Countrywide requires 30 percent of the past due payments and fees be paid before they will send you the modification agreement. In some cases, though, they have waived such a contribution. All good faith payment must be in the form of a cashier's check or a money order.

How to Process Application and Negotiate with your Lender?

Timing is important. A loan modification process can take ninety to one hundred and eighty days. To begin the process, you will first contact your lender (see chapter 19) asking if they have a package for loan modification or short sale, and whether they want you to fax or mail the package. Some lenders may have a "screener" to pre-qualify you on the phone before sending you the package so it is advisable to have your budget and hardship prepared ahead of time. Most of the items listed in chapter 16 will be required by lenders.

Once you completed your package, prepare a cover letter and fax or mail in your full package. Make sure you put all borrowers' names, property address, loan number and contact information on top of every page of every document. After about three days, call to confirm receipt of package.

It typically takes about sixty days or more to get a negotiator assigned. During this time, your lender will order a BPO to verify your LTV status, and then they will order your latest credit report. Your package is probably in an idle station waiting in line to be assigned. You will do follow up calls about once a week to check the status. If your package is incomplete, or your budget does not fit your lender's minimum requirements, you will be rejected. The clock will restart from zero every time you re-submit your file. This is why I emphasize the importance of getting everything correct the first time.

After a negotiator is assigned on your case, make sure you get his direct Email address or phone so you can follow up from time to time. The negotiator will go through your package to see if you qualify. Once he did his due diligence, he will contact you and starts the negotiation. The negotiator will only attempt to contact you a couple of times before withdrawing your application. Therefore, make sure you take his call or return his calls promptly.

First, the negotiator will ask you to confirm your information and your budget numbers. He will also want to know if the hardship is continuing, what you are doing to make improvements financially, and how much you can contribute toward the modification plan. The negotiator typically will start offering you a simple and small drop in the interest rate. You will want to ask for more, such as a principal reduction, higher drop in rates, longer amortization and/or waiving late fees, etc. As I mentioned earlier, a final agreement must benefit both parties and you must be able to make the modified payment.

Once you reached a compromise, the negotiator will go over the loan changes with you: rate, term, payment, and any deferment, etc. Make sure you clarify the contribution payment and whether there will be any attorney fees. Then you want to ask the negotiator how soon the agreement will be coming to you. Depends on each lender, in most cases, once modification terms are laid out and agreed to, the negotiator will submit the package to the investor for approval. Typically this will not be of any concern because the negotiator was negotiating with you based on guidelines set by the investor's servicing entity.

When the modification agreement arrived, all borrowers must sign and notarize. Keep a copy for your file and send the signed agreement and the cashier's check or money order back by overnight delivery. The bank typically gives you no more than two to three days deadline to sign and return.

After twenty-four hours, call the negotiator to confirm receipt of the agreement and funds. If the bank put you on a "probation" period, then make sure you follow up after you fulfilled the requirements to ask for the final agreement.

Case Studies of Modification Deals and Lenders' Guidelines

Here are examples of recent loan modification cases processed by major_lenders. The guidelines and requirements of some lenders may have changed after June 2009.

1. America's Servicing Company

Based on their general guidelines, options for loan modification are:

(a) ARM convert to fixed loan
(b) Rate reduction
(c) Term modification
(d) Payment plan
(e) On interest only loan, cannot go below market rates.

Documents required to process a loan modification are: Fax the followings:

(a) Hardship letter
(b) Financial statement
(c) Proof of income
(d) Everything must be signed and dated by borrower.

ARM Team Negotiator will be assigned and make contact.

2. American Home Mortgage Servicing Inc

AHMSI welcomes borrowers to loan modification or short sale alternatives, but normal collection and foreclosure efforts will continue uninterrupted if applicable. Files showing any deficit in the budget will be automatically declined for modification. There is no fixed requirement for the amount of surplus shown on the budget as long as there is a surplus showing. Based on their prior approved cases, it appears they require a minimum $500 surplus in order to qualify for repayment plan if in arrears.

Documents required to process a loan modification are: Fax the following to Loss Mitigation at 1-866-891-8810:

(a) A hardship letter
(b) A Financial Status Report: Fill out their Monthly Income and Expenses budget form
(c) Copy of the last two bank statements
(d) Copy of the last two pay stubs
(e) Any additional documentation to support your hardship.

Documents required to process a short sale are: Fax the following to loss mitigation at 1-866-891-8810:

(a) Listing Agreement and purchase offer
(b) Estimated HUD-1 or Estimated Net Proceeds form
(c) Proof of funds and approved financing for buyer
(d) Executed Application to Participate & Homeowner Counseling Certification (FHA insured loans only).

In one recent case, first mortgage interest rate was 7.125 percent. It was changed to a step rates: 3 percent for the first year, 3.5 percent for the second year, 4 percent for the third year, and 5 percent after the fourth year and fixed for the life of the loan. PITI payment dropped from $1,984.36 to $1,603.87. Total monthly savings between first and second mortgages was $745 per month.

In another recent case, they offered 4 percent first year, 4.5 percent second year, 5 percent third year and 6 percent for the life of the loan after that. Previous payment was interest only at $2,704, not reduced to $2,387 fully amortized.

In a third case study, AHMSI modified a loan to 4 percent the first year, 4.5 percent the second year, 5 percent the third year and 6 percent the fourth and remaining years

3. Aurora Loan Servicing

They will now verbally pre-qualify borrowers through their Loan Counseling Department. They also require a 20 percent surplus to qualify for a modification. They will most likely put you on a three month repayment plan. Anything above the 20 percent will be added into your payments for the next three months. For example, if you have $150 over the 20 percent surplus, your payment will increase by $150 for the three month repayment period. After you successfully made your second payment, you will be asked to provide your financial information and hardship letter (and bank statements if self employed).

Once all information is submitted and your third payment is made, the modification will then be finalized.

Their basic guidelines for loan modifications are:

(a) If negative amortization, will switch to fixed, but cannot end up with a deficit in budget
(b) Extend term of loan
(c) Lower interest rate
(d) Repayment plans; no principal balance reduction
(e) Loan does not have to be late to be considered.

Documents required for a loan modification are:

(a) Financial form provided by bank
(b) Two most current pay stubs (three if short sale)
(c) Hardship letter
(d) Two months of bank statement
(e) Last two years of tax returns
(f) Proof of disability, unemployment, retirement, social security
(g) Lease agreements if applicable.

4. Bank of America

Documents required for a loan modification are:

(a) Hardship letter, must be signed by all borrowers on the loan
(b) Thirty day proof of all sources of income
(c) It self employed, current profit and loss statement
(d) Taxes and insurance proof of payment, if not escrowed.

Once the complete package is submitted, the bank will need two weeks to review before it is assigned to a processor. The processor will need about 3 weeks before they get back to you.

They are now favoring the step programs, start with 2 percent to 4 percent for five years and then lock the rate for the remainder of the term at 5 percent to 5.75 percent.

In one recent case, they offered years one to five at 3.625 percent with a payment of $2,087.69, and year five through the remaining life of the loan, at 5.75 percent, with a payment of $2,526.25.

In another case, on a second mortgage, they agreed to a 75 percent payment reduction for two years from $802 to $200 at 0 percent interest. Payment then steps back up over two years. Borrower is required to make one payment at the old amount to initiate the modification.

5. Beneficial

They offer six month modification at the maximum. In one case, interest rate dropped from 13 percent to 5.25 percent, payment dropped from $615.89 to $344.49.

6. Carrington Mortgage Services

Documents required for a loan modification are:

(a) Hardship letter
(b) Two months pay stubs
(c) Two months bank statements
(d) Package provided by bank.

Once you are qualified, they will then decide on your options, most likely on lower interest rate. After the complete package is received by the bank, a negotiator will call in about seven to ten business days.

7. Chase Home Finance

Their recording message on their customer service line openly welcomes loan modifications. You can call in to make sure your package has been received and assigned. Once it is assigned you cannot get updates from the loss mitigation department. You can only get updates directly from the negotiator and they will not accept or return calls for status at all during the forty-five days of review. Chase will not work on a modification if you are in chapter 7 bankruptcy. They are so overwhelmed that they are now taking about two weeks to confirm the receipt of any fax. If the account number starts in 00, it's considered a sub-prime loan. Accounts that are not in foreclosure have to go to the Special Lending Unit (early modification team), not loss mitigation. Loss mitigation only deals with accounts in foreclosure.

Documents required for a loan modification are

(a) Two most recent pay stubs

(b) Proof of any other form of income

(c) Hardship letter.

In one recent case, interest only payment of $2,655.35 at 8.625 percent was reduced to fully amortized $1,423.12 at 3 percent the first year, $1,656.76 at 4 percent the second year, $2,063.59 at 5.625 percent the third year, and then lock in at $2,327.68 at 6.625 percent beginning fourth through life of the loan.

In a second case, Chase reduced $2,655.35 payment at 78.625 percent to $1,422.12 at 3 percent.

In a third case, original loan amount $750,000 recast in May 2008 at $825,000. They modified and offered many payment options and set a new cap amount to $862,500. They gave payment options from a minimum payment of $5,583.66 to $2,734 negative amortization (for thirty-three months) or $4,100 interest only (for ten years or until they hit the cap).

8. Citi Mortgage

Citi Mortgage announced that their preemptive "Citi Homeowner Assistance" loan modification program launched in November 2008 has helped 80,000 borrowers avoid foreclosures during the first quarter of 2009. In March 2009, the bank also launched its "Homeowner Unemployed assist" program, aimed at helping recently unemployed borrowers. This program will provide borrower three months payment forbearance so the borrower will go look for another job. This is perceived as a bridge program towards a long term solution such as a modification after borrower finds another job. To qualify for this program, the borrower must have a first mortgage owned and serviced by CitiMortagge that was conforming at the time of origination and used to finance a principal residence. The borrower must be sixty days or more delinquent on their mortgages or in foreclosure, have sufficient funds to make the reduced payment, and not be eligible in the FDIC loan modification program.

Citi has pledged another $1 billion to help borrowers refinance their existing mortgages. However, very few people qualify to get a new loan due to low or negative equity.

In anticipation of major credit card defaults, the Bank has expanded the eligibility of forbearance programs for delinquent credit card holders to tie in with the mortgage modifications. When Citi gives a homeowner a four month forbearance on the mortgage payment, the homeowner can then pay off some of the credit card debts with Citi. When those are gone, then the homeowner can afford a modified mortgage payment and allow them to stay at the home. This is a great combination which should be used by all lenders.

9. Countrywide Financial Corp

Countrywide is perhaps the most aggressive in making loan modifications since Bank of America acquired their assets at deep discounts and they had to settle many lawsuits from Attorney General of many States. They may also be the fastest in processing. Once a new file gets a verbal approval, it only gets assigned to a negotiator if it requires investor approval. Otherwise, it is processed through their automated system. If you fax your loan modification request to their work out fax number, it automatically opens modification request file, allowing you to get past the "front line" and submit information. Since most files do not get assigned to a negotiator due to their workload, it is essential that you submit your file meeting their requirement which will get you into the automated processing department.

Documents required for a loan modification are:

(a) Two months most recent pay stubs
(b) Two months most recent bank statements
(c) Last year's tax return
(d) Hardship letter which must demonstrate what caused the hardship in detail and how has it been rectified?

Their basic guidelines are:

(a) They will not do loan modification unless you are behind in your payment. However, if you can show that you have tried everything to keep up with payments but have finally run out of option, they will consider you even though you have not been late before.
(b) If you are behind in payment, then speak with the Home Retention Department, go through financials. If client qualifies, they will send request to the Workout Team. You will then send all documentations for review while a negotiator is assigned. This typically takes about thirty-five days. Once a negotiator is assigned, they will call the homeowner.
(c) If you are more than 6 months delinquent, file will go to foreclosure department. Therefore, you should start your loan modification no later than 4 months behind on your payment.
(d) Notice of Default is issued after one to two months. After sixty days, foreclosure will come into effect but it will take some time to get through foreclosure process. Any payment during that time could delay the foreclosure.

(e) To qualify for a loan modification, you must show a surplus in the budget, or at least a break-even number.

(f) Escrow accounts are typically added on for all loan modifications.

(g) Files are initially submitted verbally with a "qualifier" or "gate keeper" who will go through the financials with you and ask you general questions such as "What day of the week do you get paid?", "How many times a month do you get paid?", "How much money do you have to contribute to modification?" or "How many people living in the home?"

They are particularly aggressive on option ARM loans. They will drop rate down to 2.5 percent for five years and then step up the payment. You have to bargain hard to get a good rate locked for remainder of the term. They also initiated new programs in December 2008:

(a) Short refinancing that is not based on credit or payment history

(b) Modify negative amortization loans into fixed loans with payment that will better work for the borrower. Borrowers eligible will likely receive a letter from Countrywide advising of the programs they qualify.

As I pointed out in chapter 2, Countrywide settled charges of lending abuse and consumer fraud complaints with eleven states on an estimated $8.4 billion settlement which mostly consists of very aggressive loan modification and other relief to troubled borrowers. To qualify, your LTV must be above 75 percent and your first loan payment must be due in 2005, 2006 or 2007. You must also show a surplus after the modification.

In one recent case, Countrywide modified a negative amortization loan at 6.125 percent, $1,814.25 negative amortization payment of

$1,814.25 or interest only payment of $2,227.28 to a new interest only loan at 4.25 percent with a payment of $1,412.17 for five years.

In a second case, Countrywide modified a negative amortization loan at 5.75 percent, payment $2,780.27, down to interest only at 4.25 percent with a payment of $2,956.18 for five years.

In a third case, Countrywide offered 4.25 percent for five years, payment reduced from $2,090.43 to $1,438 per month interest only.

In a fourth case, rate dropped to 4.25 percent for five years interest only. Monthly payment dropped from $1,891.52 to $1,217.78. Total savings over sixty months is $40,424.

10. EMC Mortgage Corporation / Bear Sterns

EMC requires borrowers to go to credit counseling and attempt to consolidate their credit cards if their minimum monthly payments exceed $500 before they will consider a loan modification.

Documents required for a loan modification are:

(a) Two most recent pay stubs for each borrower
(b) Two most recent bank statements
(c) Hardship letter, demonstrating why you fell behind and what you would like to do to get caught up.

Their process is:

(a) Current on payment: File goes to Imminent Default
(b) Behind in payment, call customer service, direct them according to how far down:
    (i) Sixty days or less behind, file goes to collections,
    (ii) Sixty days or more behind goes to loss mitigation. You can do repayment plan, if you are not already in foreclosure.
(c) If already in foreclosure process, you can do forbearance plan, add to the end of the loan and get modified payment.

(d) If you are three months behind, Notice of Default can be issued. In this case, they will bend over backwards to try to make it work to prevent a foreclosure.

In one recent case, EMC dropped rate from 7.25 percent down to 5.40 percent for fifty-four months. Payment dropped from $1,743.47 to $1,309.70

In another case, rate freeze at 8.125 percent for the life of the loan on first mortgage and dropped from 12.25 percent to 2.88 percent for thirty-six months on the second mortgage.

11. <u>First Franklin Loan Services</u> (a/k/a Home Loan Services)

Documents required for a loan modification are:

(a) Financial statement
(b) Hardship letter
(c) Copies of two most recent pay stubs
(d) If self employed, six months of bank statement
(e) Verification of any other income
(f) Copy of most recent tax return. If not most recent year, copy of extension request. (g) Copy of property taxes tax bill, paid or unpaid.

They said their guidelines will not allow more than a 2 percent interest rate reduction but in one case, they allowed a 3 percent reduction.

They offer the following options:

(a) Loan modifications and repayments
(b) Once in pre-foreclosure, you will need to make at least two full payments plus 30 percent of attorney fee and other late fees.
(c) Repayment plans will take what is owed and spread it out, resulting in a payment that is doubled, or 1.50, 1.25 or 1.75.

(d) Escrow accounts are reviewed separately and can be negotiated separately.

(e) Current deficits acceptable, depends on whether the reduction in payment will create a surplus.

Once the package has been submitted, it takes seven to ten days before the file is assigned to a negotiator. Then another thirty-five to forty days before the file can be completed. Notice of Default is issued prior to ninety days delinquent. Client can make a payment prior to ninety days mark to keep home out of foreclosure process.

12. Greenpoint Mortgage

Documents required for a loan modification are

(a) Financial Statement, to be provided by bank

(b) Hardship letter

(c) Two most recent pay stubs for all borrowers

(d) If self employed, six months of profit and loss statements and matching bank statements

(e) Last year's tax return

(f) Most recent copy of property tax bills and insurance policy, if not escrowed

(g) Listing agreement if property is for sale.

There is no specific surplus requirement in your budget. Send the package for review. It will be assigned to a negotiator who will review it for feasibility and ability.

13. <u>GMAC</u>

GMAC is getting very aggressive with option ARM loans. They will reduce rates down to 1 percent for the first five years and then lock the rate at 4.5 percent for the remainder of the term.

In one recent case, original option ARM @ 6.125 percent due to recast at $4,443 per month. It was modified to 1 percent for five years fully amortized. PITI is $2,845.86 on a $712,000 loan amount.

In a second case, interest rate dropped from 7 percent to 2.5 percent for five years, PITI payment reduced from $4,472 to of $2,527.57 on a $712,000 loan amount.

In a third case, $2,509.05 payment was modified to $1,859.84 at 3 percent interest.

Documents required by loss mitigation department:

a) Financial Analysis Form
(b) Employment History
(c) Documents to verify income – Most recent tax return, and two most recent pay stubs. If commission and overtime pay are included, a letter from your employer.

For self-employed, copy of most recent profit and loss statement.

(d) Assets and Liabilities
(e) Financial Hardship Affidavit
(f) Information for Government Monitoring Purposes – ethnicity
(g) Borrower/Co-borrower Acknowledgement
(h) IRS Form 4506-T – Request for Transcript of Tax Return
(i) If you are requesting a sale of your property, a copy of the listing agreement, the sales contract and Settlement Statement if available.

14. Homecoming Financial (GMAC)

Homecoming is especially willing to work on loans that are in a negative equity situation. They will not work on loans that are current that have a fixed rate that won't be adjusting for a few years. They are willing to entertain offers for a short refinance. They typically like to see a surplus in the budget, although a break-even amount is also acceptable. If you cannot get around a deficit in the budget, you can request for a forbearance, showing that the borrower can get back on track with the bank's help, and then also ask for a modification. Modifications usually involve taking the client back to their base rate and freeze it for a period of two years. The bank will want to see consecutive payments prior to approving a modification.

Documents required for a loan modification are:

(a) Two most recent pay stubs, or other proof of income for all borrowers

(b) Two most recent bank statements, for all borrowers that contribute toward household income.

Once the package has been submitted, you can call for updates. The file will be assigned to a negotiator who will contact you. You will be told by the pre-screeners what kind of money you will have to pay to get the modification finished. If you can come up with the full amount that are behind, you can have the permanent modification expedited. Once the file is approved for modification, the bank will send out the package to the borrower for a notarized signature, and a deadline to return by. Notice of Default is issued at thirty-four days and then again at sixty-five days.

In one recent case, they agreed to waive all outstanding fees and cost but keep the same interest rate and payment.

In another case, they offered balance reduction and rate reduction to 3 percent.

15. HomEq Servicing

They typically require a three month probationary repayment plan, at the estimated reduced amount. If you successfully made those three payments, then the loan modification will be finalized. You have to get approval to submit a modification package. To get approval, you must go over all financials, hardship and have a contribution amount. They require you to come up with a contribution amount and they will counter if it's not enough. If you fit their criteria, they will forward on the reviewed information and request you fax in one month pay stub, one month bank statement, last year's tax return, and a hardship letter

In one recent case, Home Equity offered four month forbearance then lowering the rate for 5 years. Payment reduced from $3,382.12 down to $2,704.81.

16 IndyMac Federal Bank

IndyMac offers the following options:

(a) ARM modification – as long as loan is current, rate lowered 2 percent, then fixed for a period of time; cannot have budget deficit of more than $550 or a surplus of more than $1,500

(b) Normal modification – once payment is late past thirty days, they will either lower the rate or re-amortize into the principal balance. Must have a surplus of at least $100

(c) ARM resets are possible

(d) No negative amortization modification, unless within two to three months of reset, then they can possibly do reset.

Documents required for a loan modification are:

(a) Financial statement

(b) Hardship letter

(c) Most recent tax returns

(d) Most recent pay stubs

(e) If self employed, profit and loss for last two quarters

(f) Any other proof of income

(g) Everything must be signed and dated by all borrowers

Their process is:

(a) Fax the package containing the above list of documents

(b) Package will be forwarded to a negotiator. You can call for status if they have not contact you.

In one recent case, IndyMac dropped rate down to 3 percent for five years and then step up 1 percent per year until it reaches current FHA rate where it is fixed for the life of the loan. Payment went from $2,100 to $1,328.

In another case, they are using gross income to qualify the homeowner. They want the homeowner to pay at least two months of the modified amount and then at the third payment, they will review the modification for approval though there is no guarantee. On a second Home Equity line-of credit, they will do a charge off for zero interest with minimum payment arrangement until principal balance is paid off or an option for debt settlement at 70 percent off.

Please review the latest FDIC loan Modification Guidelines in this chapter which applies to IndyMac and some other defunct banks.

17. Litton Loan Servicing

Their options for loan modifications are mostly limited to lowering interest rates. Documents needed for a loan modification are:

(a) Two months of most recent bank statements
(b) Two months of most recent pay stubs
(c) Most recent tax returns
(d) Hardship letter
(e) Financial statement.

Their process is:

(a) Litton negotiators review files and issue a letter stating the reason for modification, approve or reject.
(b) Notice of Default issued thirty to forty-five days, ninety days expiration, then set up for foreclosure sale.

18 Ocwen Loan Servicing, Inc

Their guidelines are:

(a) Depends on the interest rate, the first option is to reduce the rate

(b) Depends on how long you are late on payments, the longer you are late, the more aggressive they will be willing to negotiate. It starts with loan modification options, then move into loan resolution options.

Documents required for loan modification are:

(a) Ocwen's Exhibits A, B, C and D (financial information, hardship letter, etc) and Authorization to Access Property
(b) Two most recent bank statements
(c) Two most recent pay stubs
(d) Everything must be signed and dated by all borrowers.

Their process is:

(a) Request for a package from Loan Resolution Department
(b) Fax package back with all Exhibits and conditions to Loan Resolution Department at (407) 737-5693
(c) Wait about seven days to call to go over details.

In one recent case, Ocwen dropped interest rate from 10.5 percent to 2.0 percent for five years on a second mortgage but require an upfront contribution of $644.

In another case, Ocwen dropped interest rate from 8.5 percent ARM to 6.95 percent fixed for the life of loan. Payment dropped from $780 to $526. One payment required to initiate deal and all arrears will be put to end of loan.

19. Option One

They offer the following options:

(a) Repayment plan
(b) Loan modification – incorporate past due amounts, reduce rate or term
(c) Mortgage insurance claim for one time to bring loan current
(d) Short sale or pre-foreclosure sale

(e) Deed-in-lieu of Foreclosure

If you are current on payments, they may offer loan modifications, depends on your financials and the negotiator. If you are behind in payments, they will definitely offer loan modifications. Notice of Default sent out after thirty days. Foreclosure process starts after one month but may be delayed to three, four, or five months. No deed-in-lieu of foreclosure allowed if it's not owner occupied and if it's already in foreclosure process.

Documents required for loan modification:

(a) Financial statement with budget showing at least $250 surplus
(b) Proof of income
(c) Most recent two bank statements
(d) Hardship letter.

Documents required for short sales:

(a) Most recent two months of bank statement
(b) Most recent two months of pay stubs
(c) Most recent W-2 form
(d) Hardship letter
(e) Contact name and phone number for appraisal to be completed
(f) Listing agreement with a broker
(g) Pre-approval letter for buyer without any contingencies
(h) Estimated HUD 1
(i) Signed purchase contract
(j) Put Loan # and name on top right hand corner of every page. Fax everything to 866-452-1837

Their process is:

(a) Go over financial statement on the phone. If you are qualifies, they will let you know (you can take out credit card payments in your budget to qualify if you are enrolled in debt settlement)

(b) Send package to negotiator. Write loan number, borrower's name and address on each page

(c) A negotiator will call you they he has worked through the file.

20. Saxon Mortgage Services

Loan modification is possible but hardship must be over. They will only go to the base rate. They will offer repayment if there is a surplus, repaid over maximum 7 months. Saxon is waiving late fees but charging legal fees to stop foreclosure sale if applicable. You can submit loan modification request whether you are current or behind. Options will depend on your loan status and the investor. Some investors do not allow modifications. Notice of Default expirations is thirty to sixty days.

Documents required for loan modification are:

(a) Most recent two month pay stubs for each borrower

(b) Most recent two month bank statements

(c) Most recent W-2 form

(d) Most recent tax returns

(e) Hardship letter – why you fell behind and what you would like to do to get caught up. Must show account holder names and loan number in package.

In one recent case, Saxon lowered interest rate from 11.9 percent to 6.604 percent for life of loan. Payment dropped from $1,020.93 to $684.99. Savings over one hundred and eighty months is $60,469.20.

In another case, Saxon lowered interest rate from 8.375 interest to 7 interest for five years. They required a cash contribution of $298 for attorney fees. All $27,000 arrears deferred and all late charges waived. New payment dropped from $2,877 down to $2,452.50.

21. Select Portfolio Servicing

They are only interested in loan modification if the interest rate has adjusted up or it's just about to be adjusted up. You must show a surplus in your budget. Once a plan is established, they will notify you what documentation is required.

22. Specialized Loan Servicing

They offer the following options:

(a) Principal balance reduction
(b) Extend term
(c) Lower rate.

Documents required for loan modification are:

(a) Financial statement
(b) Proof of income
(c) Hardship letter
(d) Budget must show that after modification, a minimum of 10 percent of income left over as surplus.

Their process is:

(a) Contact the Resolution Center
(b) Go over budget verbally with a screener on the phone
(c) Prepare package, adjust financial statement to fit verbal communication with the screener's request
(d) Fax the package
(e) A negotiator will be assigned and contact you.

In one recent case regarding a second lien mortgage by SLS, they agreed to a three month forbearance, dropped interest rate from 10.875 percent to 7 percent, reduced payment from $716.60 to $503.76.

23. <u>U.S. Bank</u> (Wilshire Capital)

In one recent case, they dropped interest rate from 7.5 percent down to 5.5 percent fixed for life of loan. Payment dropped from $1,835.44 down to $1,466.96.

24. Wachovia (now Citi Bank)

Wachovia is more interested in offering short term forbearances of one to three months and refinancing instead of loan modification. Modifications are possible, but only after the payment plans are done. Here are some of their guidelines:

(a) For a repayment plan, if you are behind by only two – three months, you must make at least one payment as good faith, then the next two months can be spread out over the next two months.

(b) If you are behind more than three months, you will be required to make enough of a good faith payment to get within two payments of being back on track before they are willing to work on a plan.

(c) On a primary residence, the bank can work with high debt ratios. If it is not your primary residence, the highest ratio they will go is 55 percent.

Their process is:

(a) The initial interview involves going over the financials and explaining the hardship. If you are asking for a modification or repayment plan and you are behind on payments, the bank will want to know how much money you can contribute toward the plan.

(b) Once the initial interview is done, a negotiator will be assigned to review and request all need documentation, such as proof of income. They will also be pulling your credit report and doing a property report. When a negotiator calls you, you must respond within twenty-four hours or your file will be closed.

(c) After documentation has been reviewed, the bank will send a package for you to sign (notarized) and requesting for your money order sent back within a few days.

In one recent case, they offered to write down 20 percent of the loan amount, extend the borrower's term to forty years with a 10 year interest only. The 20 percent will not be added as a silent second; it is written off. The bank is also forgiving any past due unpaid interest.

25. Washington Mutual, Inc

WaMu seems to require at least thirty days past due before considering any loan modification. On a short sale, if they hold the first mortgage, they will give a maximum of $5,000 to the second mortgage lender. If your file is transferred to a new negotiator, their review time (thirty to ninety days) will start all over regardless of how long the previous negotiator had the file. Your budget surplus or deficit must be within one half of your payment amount to be qualified for loan modification consideration. For example, if your mortgage payment is $1,800 a month, your budget must be within $900 surplus or $900 deficit to be qualified. They offer loan modifications and repayment plans.

Documents required for loan modification are:

(a) Financial statement
(b) Hardship letter
(c) Budget
(d) Most recent bank statements
(e) Most recent pay stubs
(f) Most recent tax returns with all schedules. If current year return was extended, show a copy of the extension.

In one recent case, WaMu approved a step program with a rate of 3.329 percent the first year, 4.223 percent the second year, then 5.208 percent the third year and lock in for remainder of the term. The original interest rate was 6.193 percent. Escrow impounds of approximately $288.15 were added to the payment.

In another case, WaMu approved 3 percent first year, 4.29 percent second year, then 5.5 percent the third year and locked for life of loan. Term extended to four hundred and forty-nine months. Payment dropped from $2,643 interest only down to $1,465 fully amortized. Upfront contribution of $408 in certified funds required. All arrears put to the back of the loan.

26. Wells Fargo Home Mortgage

Wells Fargo will work with clients in bankruptcy as long as you get a release from the bankruptcy lawyer. They say their guidelines cannot do loan modification more than 2 percent interest rate reduction but they frequently agreed to modifications better than that. They also say they do not work on borrowers who are not behind in their payments. Even if the borrower indicated they have a negative cash flow, they believe they will find a way to make payments because so far they have been able to do so. On an interest only loan, their floor rate is 2 percent, but on a P & I loan, they will go to 0 percent if needed, but the borrower has to show a surplus or they will be disqualified for any loan modification.

Their basic guidelines are:

(a) FHA loans can do a Partial Claim (0 percent interest loan for unpaid balance that is paid off when home is sold, refinanced or paid in full) for those who can continue making payments.

(b) If you are anticipating a deficit for a short time, they will allow you to defer payment up to ninety days, but the loan must be brought current at the end of ninety days.

(c) You can show a current deficit but you must show a surplus after modification. (d) Will switch ARM to a fixed rate.

(e) Will lower interest rate.

(f) Will extend term.

(g) Amount past due can be recapped onto the end of the loan.

(h) Repayment plan will spread payment out over twelve months.

(i) No deferment.

(j) Will not modify investment properties or interest only loans

Documents required for loan modification are:

(a) Proof of income

(b) Hardship letter

(c) Monthly budget.

In one recent case, Wells Fargo Agreed to write down a $1,170,000 principal balance down to $700,000, lower the interest rate and extend the term. Additionally, they will forbear the write down amount.

In a second case, Wells Fargo dropped interest rate from 7.99 percent to 5 percent for five years. Payment dropped from $3,890.13 down to $2,434.75.

In a third case, Wells Fargo offered a partial claim through HUD at 0 percent interest to bring the borrower current. The loan will not be paid on until the house has been paid off.

In a forth case, Wells Fargo approved a partial claim for all the past due balance after completing a three month repayment plan. There is a contribution requirement of $2,546.76 to cover attorney fees and some late charges but they will accept this in payments as long as borrower agrees they owe the amount. The borrower was given a silent second with HUD at 0 percent interest for the past due balance of $23,542.14 (10 months behind). No payments are due on this loan until the first is paid off.

27. Wilshire Credit Corporation

Documents required for loan modifications:

(a) Financial Statement – use their form.

(b) Most recent two pay stubs or last thirty days.

(c) Bank statements.

(d) Most recent tax returns.

(e) W-2s

(f) Letter of Explanation – hardship.

All submission must be in writing, no verbal submission.

The above case studies provide you a good insiders' view of what major lenders have agreed so far, or what their basic guidelines on loan modifications. It is important to point out that these are simply some selected cases completed by major banks, and their guidelines at the time. Lenders are known to keep changing their rules but, fortunately in most cases, they are now more aggressive and more willing to settle for lower rates and lower payments than ever before. Even if a lender has a set guideline, they are known to bend the rules to make some cases work. Therefore, even if the above cases settled at rates or terms less than your expectation, you may still be able to achieve what you needed, within reason. Again, I must emphasize the end solution must be to the benefit of both parties, not just you. If you are qualified under the Home Affordable Modification program discussed in chapter 13, please refer to that paragraph for specific requirements.

FDIC Loan Modification Guidelines

The Federal Deposit Insurance Corporation (FDIC) has initiated a systematic loan modification program at IndyMac Federal Bank to reduce first lien mortgage payments to as low as 31 percent of monthly income. Modifications are based on interest rate reductions, extension of term, and principal forbearance. These guidelines are somewhat similar to the Home Affordable Loan Modification program. It also provides incentives to the lender by:

(a) Paying servicers $1,000 to cover expenses for each loan modified according to the required guidelines; and
(b) Sharing up to 50 percent of losses incurred if a modified loan should subsequently re-default. .

Here are the Guidelines:

1. This program is also limited to owner occupied properties.
2. Government loss sharing would be available only after the borrower has made six modified payments.
3. A net present value test will be used to compare foreclosing versus modification to assure the lender is better off to do modification. This test will determine the nets present value of the modified loan, as compared to the projected amount of recoveries obtained in the disposition by short sale or foreclosure. All participating lenders will be required to apply the same test on all its loans and they must carry out the modification if the result indicates a modification provides a better result than foreclosure.
4. For loans with LTV above 100 percent, the government loss share will be progressively reduced from 50 percent to 20 percent as the current LTV rises. If the LTV for the first lien mortgage exceeds 150 percent, no loss sharing would be provided.

Chapter 19: Lenders' Contact Information

1. Accredited Home Lenders
   Address: 15253 Avenue of Science, Bldg 3, San Diego, CA 92128
   Primary phones: 877-273-4599 or 877-683-4466
   Primary fax: 866-703-6318
   Loss Mitigation phone: 866-551-3894
   Website/Email (Loan Modification): www.accredhome.com
   Hours: 8 am – 10 pm
2. Acqura Loan Services
   Primary phone: 866-660-5804
   Website/Email: www.acqura.net
3. America's Servicing Company
   Address: 7495 New Horizon Way, Frederick, MD 21703
   Primary phone: 866-248-5719
   Primary fax: 866-590-8910
   Loss Mitigation Phone: 877-222-7875 ext 4

Loss Mitigation Fax: 866-590-8910

ARM team: 866-398-7569

When faxing, put attention: Correspondence Department and list loan no.

Hours: 8 am – 9 pm CST. Monday -Thursday; 8 am to 8 pm Friday.

4. American Home Mortgage Servicing, Inc

   Address: P. O. Box 631730, Irving, Texas 75063-1730

   Primary phones: 877-304-3100 (Option 5) or 877-374-3100

   Primary fax: 949-790-8505

   Loan Workout Department: 877-304-3100 - (need to get negotiator's extension once assigned)

   Loss Mitigation fax: 866-891-8810

   Website/Email: www.online.ahmsi3.com

   Hours: Monday – Friday 7 am – 7 pm CST

5. Aurora Loan Services

   Address: 3617 College Park, P.O. Box 1706, Scottsbluff, NE 69363-1706

   Primary phones: 800-550-0508 or 866-519-3090

   Home retention phone: 866-521-3828

   Loss Mitigation fax: 866-517-7976

   Website/Email: www.myauroraloan.com

   Hours: Monday through Thursday 8 am – 11 pm, Friday 8 am – 9 pm,

   Saturday 8 am – 4 pm, EST.

6. Avelo Mortgage

   Primary phone: 800-999-8501

   Website/Email: www.littonloan.com

7. Bank of America

   Address: 475 Crosspoint Parkway, P.O. Box 9000, Getzville, N. Y. 14068-9000

Primary phones: 800-285-6000 or 800-846-2222
Primary fax: 716-635-2600
Assumptions/Home Retention: 716-365-7256
Loss Mitigation Fax: 716-635-7255
Website/Email: www.bankofamerica.com

8. Beneficial
   Primary phone: 800-371-6441
   Loss Mitigation phone: 800-340-7505
   Website/Email: www.beneficial.com

9. Carrington Mortgage Services
   Primary phones: 800-561-4567 or 800-790-9502
   Primary faxes: 949-517-5220 or 866-251-4563
   Website/Email: myloan.carringtonms.com

10. Chase Home Finance
    Address: 10790 Rancho Bernardo Road, San Diego, CA 92127
    P. O. Box 24573, Columbus, OH 43224
    Primary phones: 800-548-7912 or 866-550-5705
    Loss Mitigation phone: 877-838-1882
    Loss Mitigation Fax: 888-219-7813
    Collections fax: 877-383-1563
    Hours: Monday – Friday 8 am – 9 pm, Saturday 8 am – 5 pm EST
    Website/Email: www.chase.com

11. Citi Bank
    Primary phone: 800-401-6587
    Primary fax_ 856-988-5185

12. Citi Residential Lending (Citigroup, Inc, Citi Mortgage)
    Primary phones: 800-430-5262 or 866-915-9417

Primary fax: 949-862-3526, attention: Correspondence Department

Website/Email: www.citigroup.com/citi/citizen/community/homeownershipprservation.com

13. Countrywide Home Loans

    Address: Customer Service, SVB 314, P. O. Box 5170, Simi Valley, CA 93062-5170. For overnight: 400 Countrywide Way, Semi Valley, CA 93065.

    Primary phone: 800-669-0102

    Foreclosure Dept "Home Retention Team" phone: 800-669-6650

    Foreclosure Dept "Home Retention Team" fax: 800-658-0395

    Website/Email: www.countrywide.com

    Hours: Monday – Thursday 8 am – 9 pm, Friday 8 am – 5 pm,

    Saturday 8 am – 1 pm PST

14. EMC Mortgage Corporation / Bear Sterns

    Address: P. O. Box 293150, Lewisville, TX 75029-3150

    Primary phones: 800-723-3004 or 866-550-5705

    Loan Workout Department phones: 888-577-4011 or 866-564-3529

    Imminent Default phone: 866-418-5901

    Loss Mitigation Fax: 917-849-2677 or 214-626-4706

    Website/Email: emcmortgagecorp.com

    Once you have a negotiator assigned, you can request their direct extension, fax number and email address.

    Hours: Monday – Thursday 7 am – 11 pm, Friday 7 am – 7 pm CST

15 First Franklin Loan Services (a/k/a Home Loan Services)

    Address: IDC 24-120, Loss Mitigation, 150 Allegheny Center Mall, Pittsburgh, PA 15212

Primary phone: 800-622-5035

Primary fax: 724-957-9032

Loan Workout Department phone: 800-622-5035, Assistance Counselor extension 11854

Loss Mitigation faxes: 412-918-7340, 412-918-7307, or 412-918-7336

Hours: Best contact time 8 am – 4 pm EST

16 First Horizon Home Loans

Primary phone: 800-364-7662

Website/Email: www.firsthorizon.com

Franklin Loan Services & NationPoint Loan Services

Primary phone: 800-500-5022

Website: www.viewmyloan.com and www.nationpoint.com

17 Greenpoint Mortgage

Address: P. O. Box 84013, Columbus, GA 31908-4013

2300 Brookstone Center Parkway, Columbus, GA 31904

Primary phone: 800-784-5566

Primary fax: 706-641-4453

Loss Mitigation Department: 800-784-5566, ext 5371, ext 5383 and ext 3418

Loss Mitigation Fax: 415-878-4895

Hours: Monday – Friday 8 am – 5 pm EST

18 GMAC

Address: Customer Care Correspondence Unit, P. O. Box 780, Waterloo, IA 50704-0780

Address: Loss Mitigation, 2711 North Haskell Ave., Suite 900, Dallas, TX 75204

Primary phones: 800-766-4622 or 800-799-9250

Loan Servicing phone: 866-725-0782

Loss Mitigation phone: 800-800-4622

Loss Mitigation fax: 1-866-709-4744

Website/Email: www.gmacmortgage.com
Hours: Monday – Friday 6 am – 10 pm and Saturday 9 am – 1 pm, CST

19 Golden 1 Credit Union
Primary phone: 916-732-2900
Primary fax: 916-455-5165

20 Great Basin
Primary phone: 775-333-4228
Primary fax: 775-789-3160

21 Homecomings/GMAC
Address: 3451 Hammond Avenue, Waterloo, IA 50702
Primary phone: 800-206-2901
Primary fax: 800-211-3561
Loss Mitigation Department: 800-799-9250, need to get direct extension once a negotiator is assigned.
Loss Mitigation faxes: 866-340-5043 or 800-211-3561
Website/Email: www.homecomings.com
Hours: Monday – Thursday 7 am – 9 pm, Friday 8 am – 6 pm,
Saturday 8 am – 12 pm CST.

22 HomEq Servicing
Primary phone: 877-867-7378
Website/Email: www.homeq.com

23 HSBC Finance (HSBC Consumer Lending)
Primary phone: 800-333-5848
Website/Email: www.hfc.com

24 HSBC Finance (HSBC Mortgage Services)
Primary phone: 800-365-6730
Website/Email: www.hsbcmortgageservices.com

25 HSBC Mortgage Corporation

Primary phone: 888-648-3124
Website/Email: www.us.hsbc.com

26 IndyMac Federal Bank
Address: 7700 Parmer Lane, Bldg. D, Second Floor, Austin, TX 78729
Primary phones: 877-736-5556 or 866-355-7273
Loss Mitigation phone: 877-736-5556
Loss Mitigation fax: 626-583-1370
Website/Email: www.imb.com
Hours: Monday – Friday 8 am – 9 pm EST

27 Litton Loan Servicing
Address: 4828 Loop Central Drive, Houston, TX 77081
Primary phones: 800-548-8665 or 800-999-8501
Primary fax: 713-218-3777 or 713-218-3716
Customer Service (if payment is current): 800-548-8665
Collection Department (if payment is late): 800-999-8601
Loss Mitigation phone: 800-247-9727
Loss Mitigation fax: 713-218-3525
Foreclosure Department phone: 800-247-9727
Website/Email: www.littonloan.com
Hours: 8 am – 5 pm CST

28 LoanCare Servicing Center
Primary phones: 800-909-9525 or 800-274-6600
Website/Email: www.myloancare.com/HomeRetention
customersupport@myloancare.com

29 MedLife Homes
Primary phone: 800-922-6267
Website/Email: www.metlifehomeloans.com

30 National City Mortgage Corporation
Primary phones: 800-523-8654 or 888-622-4932

Loss Mitigation Department phone: 877-526-3603
Primary fax: 269-973-2131
Website/email: www.nationalcitymortgage.com

31 Nationstar Mortgage, LLC
Primary phone: 888-480-2432
Primary fax: 972-315-6968
Website/Email: customer.service@nationstarmail.com

32 Ocwen Loan Servicing, LLC
Address: 12650 Ingenuity Drive, Orlando, FL 32826
Primary phones: 877-596-8580 or 800-310-9229
Primary fax: 407-737-6300
Loss Mitigation phone: 800-746-2936
Loan Resolution Department: 888-779-2857 or 407-737-5693
Loss Mitigation fax: 407-737-5693
Website/Email: www.ocwencustomers.com
Hours: Monday – Friday 8 am – 6 pm EST

33 Option One
Address: P. O. Box 57054, Irvine, CA 92619
Primary phone: 800-704-0800
Primary fax: 949-790-8505
Home Retention Department phones: 888-275-2648 or 877-304-3100
Loss Mitigation fax: 866-669-3671
Short Sale fax: 866-452-1837
Hours: Monday – Friday 5 am – 9 pm PST

34 Residential Credit Solutions
Primary phone: 800-737-1192
Website/Email: www.residentialcredit.com

35 RoundPoint mortgage Servicing Corporation

Primary phone: 877-426-8805

Website/Email: Customer.Service@roundpointmortgage.com www.roundpointmortgage.com

36 Saxon Mortgage Services

Primary phones: 888-325-3502 or 800-594-8422

Primary fax: 817-665-7970

Loan Workout Department: 888-325-3502, need to get negotiator's extension once assigned.

Loss Mitigation fax: 888-240-1885

Website/Email: www.saxononline.com

Hours: Monday – Friday 7 am – 10 pm, Saturday 7 am – 2 pm.

37 Select Portfolio Servicing, Inc.

Address: P. O. Box 65250, Salt Lake City, UT 84165-0250

Primary phone: 800-258-8602

Primary fax: 801-269-4399

Loss Mitigation Department phone: 800-258-8602

Loan Resolution phone: 888-818-6032

Website/Email: www.spservicing.com

Hours: Monday – Friday 7 am – 8 pm, Saturday 8 am – 12 pm EST

38 Specialized Loan Servicing

Address: 8742 Lucent Blvd;, Suite 300, Highland Ranch, CO 80129

Primary phone: 800-315-4757

Customer Care Modification phone: 800-306-6062

Primary fax: 720-241-7526

Resolution Center phone: 800-306-6059

Hours: Monday – Friday 5 am – 8 pm MST

39 Suntrust Mortgage, Inc.

Primary phones: 800-634-7928 or 800-443-1032 (option 3)

Primary fax: 804-291-0748
Loan Workout Department: 800-443-1032
Loss Mitigation Fax: 804-675-9737
Website/Email: www.suntrustmortgage.com
Hours: Monday – Friday 8 am – 5 pm EST

40 SunTrust Mortgage Home Equity
Primary phone: 888-886-0696
Website/Email: equityhomeretention@suntrust.com
www.suntrustmortgage.com

41 SunTrust Mortgage Construction/Permanent Loans
Primary phone: 877-657-8433
Website/Email: www.suntrustmortgage.com

42 Taylor, Bean & Whitaker
Primary phone: 888-225-2164
Website/Email: www.taylorbean.com

43 The CIT Group/Consumer Finance, Inc
Primary phone: 800-225-2164
Website/Email: citcares@cit.com

44 Wachovia / World Savings
Address: P. O. Box 60505, Industry, CA 91716
Primary phones: 800-922-6267 or 800-642-0257
Primary fax: 210-509-1174
Loss Mitigation phone: 800-282-3451
Loan Resolution Center (for modifications of delinquent loans, not ARMs)
Phones: 866-290-8954
Website/Email: www.wachovia.com
Hours: 8 am – 5 pm CST

45 Washington Mutual, Inc.

Address: Loss Mitigation / Default Alternatives (JAX A2000) Department,

7255 Baymeadows Way, Jacksonville, FL 32256

Primary phones: 866-926-8937 or 866-550-5705

Primary fax: 818-775-2591

Loss Mitigation phones: 866-378-6582, 866-926-8937 or 800-918-4029

Loss Mitigation faxes: 904-886-1328, 469-948-9461, 904-886-5529, or 904-886-6253

Behind on payments 469-549-5608, Current 206-926-6910

Website/Email: www.wamu.com

Hours: Collections – Monday – Thursday 5 am – 9 pm, Friday 5 am – 6 pm,

Saturday 5 am – 2 pm, Sunday 12 pm – 9 pm.

Loss Mitigation – Monday – Friday 8 am – 6 pm, Saturday 12 pm – 9 pm,

Sunday 11 am – 5 pm.

46 Wells Fargo Home Mortgage

Address: P. O. Box 10368, Des Moines, IA 50306-0368

Primary phones: 800-222-0238 or 866-488-2028

Primary fax: 866-917-1877

Loss Mitigation Department phone: 877-216-8448 (if behind on payments)

Adjustable Rate Team phone: 866-398-7567 (if current on payments)

Loss Mitigation fax: 866-359-7363

Website/Email: www.wellsfargo.com

Hours: Monday – Friday 8 am – 10 pm, Friday 8 am – 9 pm

47 Wells Fargo Financial

Primary phone: 800-275-9254

Website/Email: financial@wellsfargo.com

48 Wilshire Credit Corporation
Address: P. O. Box 8517, Portland, OR 97207 (attention: Modification)
Primary phone: 888-502-0100
Loss Mitigation phone: 888-917-1050
Loss Mitigation faxes: 503-525-7229 or 503-946-3848

Some Tricks on Contacting a Negotiator

Sometimes it is very hard to get through the main lines to the loss mitigation department or it's hard to get pass the "gate keeper" or "screener". You may have left a bunch of messages but no one calls you back. If you are desperately needing to contact your negotiator but do not have his/her direct contact, there are a few tricks you can try. Every negotiator, possibly everyone for that matter, communicates through emails. All lenders have a set Email address structure for all employees. If you still have the business card of your loan officer, it will give you a place to start. Another way to detect the structure is visit your lender's web site and look for "Contact Us" Email structure. You can also try to ask for loan (make them feel like you are a new customer) and get a contact person's email address. If they want your business, they will be more than likely to give you an email address which will help you break the code. For example, Chase Home Finance email structure is joseph.b.smith@Chase.com, Countrywide email structure is Joe_Smith@Countrywide.com, IndyMac email structure is Joe.Smith@imb.com, and some banks email structure are JSmith@bank.com. There are only a few common structures so it does not take long that you can figure out your lender's email structure. If you have the name of the person you want to contact, then you have a good chance of coming up the correct email address. After all, if you are wrong, your email will simply be returned to you. If you do not have a name, then you may need to sweet talk the "gate keeper" receptionist to give you a name. Once you break the code and get to the person, make sure you respect that person and be nice in presenting yourself. Otherwise, they may block your email address or never respond to you.

Aside from breaking email codes, you can even try to break a phone number code. Most major banking center use one large block of consecutive phone numbers for all departments. Once you get one phone number of that department you try to reach, you can randomly try dialing numbers + or – 1 through 20 from the number you have. Each time you reached someone at the bank, find out what department you reached. You can try apologizing for dialing the wrong department and ask for the correct number or switching to the correct department for you. Always be courteous and sweet; it will get you where you want to reach. Even if you get the correct contact phone number, do not call too frequent that will become annoying. All loss mitigation negotiators are extremely busy. They do not want to spend a lot of time on the phone with you. However, it is utmost important that if the negotiator do contact you, you must be available to answer his/her call immediately.

Your initial contact will be with one of the following departments: Loss Mitigation (the most common), Homeowner Retention, Asset Management or Loan Work out. First ask if they have a specific package for loan modification or whatever other options you want to pursue. If so, then ask them to email the package to you (which may also help you break their email structure code). In most cases, you will be asked to fax in the required documents as discussed in chapter 18.

Chapter 20 Debt Settlement

How to Reduce your Credit Card Debts?

Debt Settlement or Debt Negotiation is another form of loan modification. It applies to mostly unsecured debts such as credit cards, personal loans, medical bills, etc. Business credit card debts can be included only if the business is closed. Secured debts such as mortgage loans, auto loans, IRS debts, lawsuits, judgments, government loan, student loan, etc will not qualify. Although debt settlement is typically done separately, it can be incorporated as part of your overall budget cutting solution in loan modification. Mortgage lenders actually welcome you to enroll in the debt settlement program because it tells them you are willing to give up your credit cards in order to keep your house. During the hard times, people tend to rely on credit cards to bridge their deficit and, before long, they max out their credit card limits and unable to survive. Then when you are accumulated too much debt or unable to make the minimum payments, banks start pushing up your interest rates to ridiculously high levels as much as 29.99 percent per annum and, at the same time, they will eliminate your remaining credit lines. Once that happens, you entered a point of no return. In the second quarter of 2009, the Federal Reserve's survey of major lenders showed 65 percent had lowered the credit limits of existing customers. The Federal Reserve also reported that total U. S. revolving debts is now over $850 billion. It has expanded by almost 50 percent in 2008. Average American household now has over $10,700 in credit card debts. Even as the economy worsens, credit card issuers sent out 4.2 billion credit card offers in the mail in 2008. This is because the average return on equity for banks specialized in credit cards was 15.1 percent as compared to 8.2 percent for banks in general, according to FDIC data for 2007.

Like the mortgage loan modification business, the debt settlement industry has grown by leaps and bounds in the past few years. There is no license required to do debt settlement and the industry is by far unregulated. Texas, California and Florida have the highest concentration of debt settlement companies. Financially distressed consumers have flocked to the debt settlement companies. Many of them are scam operations but some are legitimate. Among the legitimate ones, many are nothing more than marketing lead generators who will simply turn you over to the real debt settlement companies and earn a commission. Please refer to chapter 6 to review the basic rules on how to avoid a scam. Make sure you check the number of complaints filed with the BBB. You can also look up The Association of Settlement Companies (TASC) and International Association of Professional Debt Arbitrators. Members of these organizations have to abide by certain guidelines and they also have an accredited program. However, just being a member does not guarantee they are good and honest.

Like loan modification, you do not have to engage a consultant to negotiate with your credit card companies. You can do it yourself but it may be difficult and stressful talking to the collection department or a collection agency. Once your payment is over ninety days late, your bank is likely to sell your bad debts to a collection agency at a deep discount. The collection agencies have trained professionals to harass you non-stop and they will threat you with all kinds of legal actions until you give in and accept their offer of a "discounted" payment. Debt collectors' use tactics to "press your button" to the edge so you will become annoyed and pay your bill. When the debt collector start making you offers to settle for a discount, you can use the opportunity to negotiate for a better deal yourself and save the fees you have to pay a debt settlement company. A professional debt settlement company, however, can usually negotiate a bigger discount in the neighborhood of 50 percent off and they will not engage into an emotionally fight like you would.

Before you consider this route, I urge you to think it over very carefully or visit a free HUD approved credit counseling center (see chapter 8) for advice. Debt Settlement should be the last resort for you before bankruptcy.

Potential Problems Associated with Debt Settlement

There are many possible problems associated with debt settlement:

1 There is no guarantee any of your creditors will agree to a settlement.

2 Creditors may choose to pursue legal action against you. They may file a lawsuit and obtain a judgment against you for the amount owed plus any interest or fees awarded by the judge. Then they can file an Abstract of Judgment in the County Clerk's Office which will become a public record. If you ever

try to sell a non-homestead exempt real property in your name, the judgment plus any awarded interest and fees will have to be paid in full to obtain a release or you will not be able to sell that property. The judgment will also empower the creditors to garnish your bank accounts and remove money from them without your consent.

3 The "savings" from settlement of your credit cards may be smaller than the fees you are paying the debt settlement company.

4 Your credit will be ruined once your credit cards are seriously late in payment. It will stay on your credit report of seven years.

5 Enroll in a debt settlement program will not stop the non-stop harassment from the collection agencies.

6 If you enrolled in a scam debt settlement operation, not only they will take the money from you, no one is negotiating with your creditors. Your credit will be ruined for nothing. You can find some of the complaint reported on debt settlement companies on BBB's web site. In one case, a person got so upset he gave up after sending money for over a year to a debt settlement company. Not only did he not getting any debt settled, he was sued by the creditors.

7 Forgiven portion of the debts may become your taxable income.

8 It may take as long as three years to get all your credit card debts settled, depends on the total amount of debts enrolled and the amount you can afford to pay into the program each month.

9 Sometimes you may get lucky that when your bad debt was sold by your lender to a collection agency, the paperwork may

get lost or mistakes were made in the record. Keep in mind that you have the right to ask for written proof of your debt, particularly if any statement you received from the collection agency shows incorrect account number or a debt that is more than two years old. This is known as "validation of debt". If they fail to show you proof that they own your debt, they must halt their collection efforts against you. You may just get away with 100 percent of your debt before enrolling in any debt settlement program. However, without a settlement, those debts will stay on your credit report as debts unpaid. You should only challenge validation of debt against the debt collection agencies but not against your lender who is likely to keep all the original records.

Debt Settlement Process – Step by Step

If you are already in such a bad shape that you have no alternative but to enroll in a debt settlement program, then let me walk you through how the debt settlement companies work before you enroll:

1. Most debt settlement companies require a minimum of $10,000 of unsecured debts to be enrolled in the program. The average amount in the industry is $50,000 of debts.
2. You do not have to enroll every one of your credit cards. You may choose to keep one or two for your convenient use. However, once the seriously past due cards start showing up on your credit report, your remaining cards may be facing with lower limits or even be terminated without being behind in payments.
3. There is no credit check. You do not have to own a home.

4. Upon enrollment, the debt settlement companies will require you to stop making any payment on those cards or debts. This is why banks will do everything to discourage you from enrolling in the programs. Credit counseling agencies will strongly discourage you defaulting payments on purpose while you are still able to make the minimum payments. This may be construed as another form of loan fraud and some lenders may take you to court. Some banks are willing to negotiate directly with you with some kind of payment plan and waive the high interest or late fees if you tell them your only alternative is to enroll in a debt settlement program. You should try to do this before they sell your loan to collection agencies at pennies on the dollar. That usually happens when you are ninety to one hundred and eighty days late.

5. Once you are late in your payments, you will get frequent calls from your lender. Then when your lender sold your bad debt to a collection agency, the collection agents will harass you non-stop, days and nights. They have ways to find you, even if you change your numbers. Collectors do have to abide by the laws of the Fair Debt Collection Practices Act. Most state laws prohibit debt collectors from doing the following:
   (a) Calling you at home before 8 am or after 9 pm;
   (b) Calling you at your work after you have told them you cannot receive such calls;
   (c) Telling your neighbor, co-worker or non-spouse that you owe money;
   (d) Calling an excessive number of times;
   (e) Continue to call after receiving written request to stop;
   (f) Threatening violence, arrest or incarceration;
   (g) Using profanity or harassing and abusive language;
   (h) Threatening to take your house or garnish your wages.

Once you enrolled in a debt settlement program, you can write the collection agency a letter to inform them that you are enrolled and all future communications should be directed through that company. This may help stop the calls because they know once you enrolled in a debt settlement program, they will end up negotiating with the settlement company and they will be wasting time to continue harassing you to pay. However, there is no guarantee they will leave you alone. The most effective way is to engage a lawyer (or get a lawyer friend to do you a favor?) to write them a letter demanding all future communication to go through your lawyer. It will stop the calls and, trust me, they will not call or harass your lawyer. Also, it has become increasingly popular to file a lawsuit against the collection agency. A lot of consumers do not know they can go after the debt collectors. In fact they can even get paid for their pain and recover all their legal fees. In one recent case, debt collectors relentlessly called a Texas woman while her husband was in Iraq, threatening her that she would lose her freedom, her house, and her children if she does not pay her debt; and she would go to jail. It was so brutal and horrifying that she finally consulted an attorney to sue. At the end, she got $17,500 under the federal Fair Debt Collection Practice Act and over $50,000 in legal fees and costs reimbursed. Texas is especially famous for two multimillion-dollar cases under the laws to curb debt collectors. Trying to get $2,700 owed on a Visa card bill, collectors swore at an El Paso couple, harassed them at work, and said they would put out a contract to kill one of them and even called a bomb threat to one of their workplace. A jury awarded the couple $11 million, though an appeals court cut that down to $1 million in 1998. In another famous case, an elderly woman was awarded $15 million after being harangued about a relative's debt. You can sue either under the state or federal law. Not all debt collectors are like the examples listed here. You cannot sue just to get away from paying. The debt collector must have violated the law before you take this drastic step. If you are a victim, you can file your complaint to the Federal Trade Commission or your state Attorney General's Office.

6. Most debt settlement companies charge 15 percent fee on the amount of the debts enrolled into the program in non-restricted states like Texas and California. Twenty-three states have restrictions that cap the fee at 10 percent and require it to go through an attorney. However, companies in those restricted states typically add on a monthly fee in addition to their 10 percent fee. Some companies will charge you a one time set up fee like $199. Therefore, if you enroll $40,000 debts into the program, your total fee payable to the debt settlement company will be somewhere from $6,000 to $7,000. Most companies will allow you to spread out the fees into twelve to eighteen months so you do not have to pay them upfront, but that will only delay the time they start negotiate with your creditors. None of your debts will be settled until you have paid their fees.
7. Once you enrolled in a program, the settlement company will ask you to prepare a budget and determine a fixed amount each month you can set aside to settle these debts. Then you will set up a Trust savings account in your name, which can be at your bank but usually at a bank they designated. Each month you will make one single deposit of a fixed amount into that account. During the initial six to twelve months, money in your account will first apply to their fees. After you fulfilled paying their fees, then your account will start showing surpluses. When the surpluses accumulates, then they will start negotiate with the first creditor. When a creditor agreed to a settled amount, usually about 40 percent to 60 percent (some claim they can save you as much as 70 percent) below what you owed, they will pay that amount out of your account and closed that deal.

Then they will wait until your account builds up sufficient funds again before negotiate with the second creditor. This process will repeat one creditor at a time until all your debts are settled and paid. This can easily take three years, depends on the amount of debts enrolled and the amount of payment you can afford to make each month. Settlement companies typically tell you the minimum enrollment is twelve month to eighteen months but in reality, it usually takes much longer. They do not start negotiating with any creditor until they get their fees and your account start accumulated enough money to settle. Also, they do not allow you to cancel prior to the minimum enrollment period.

8. The benefit of debt settlement goes beyond the typical 40 percent to 60 percent of your debts forgiven is that it will also save you a lot of interest.
9. For those debts that you have settled, it will show on your credit report as either "settled in full" or "settled in reduced amount".

What are the Tax Consequences

After settlement, creditors typically will send you a 1099-C Cancellation of Debt tax form for the portion of debts forgiven since they have to report how they write off a receivable. Consult with your accountant or check out IRS's Insolvency Exclusion guidelines (Publication 4681, www.IRS.gov) which allow you to exclude the forgiven debt as income if you were insolvent immediately before debt cancellation. Insolvency is defined by IRS as the "total of all of your liabilities exceeded the fair market value of all of your assets". Assets include the value of everything you own, including those collateralized or exempt from creditors. Liabilities include all recourse debts and non-recourse debts that are not in excess of the fair market value of the property that is security for the debt.

What is Debt Consolidation?

Debt Consolidation is totally different from debt settlement or credit repairs. Debt Consolidation involves a new loan to pay off all your other debts so you will be making one single payment. Most debt consolidation loans are home equity loans, secured by a second lien mortgage on your home. Interest rate could be higher than the average of the debts you are paying off. It may not be worth the fees just for the convenience of making one single payment. You are also giving up unsecured debts for a secured debt which may cause you to lose your house if you are unable to pay. It may even cause your credit score to go down if you cancel all the credit cards that you are paying off. I will discuss that in chapter 31.

Credit Card Reform Act 2009

As credit card defaults keep on rising rapidly, credit card lenders started to increase rates drastically, tag on huge fees, and cut off balances without any advance notice. Consumers are being hit with shocking surprises and embarrassing declines when they try to make a credit card purchase thinking they have plenty of credit left remaining. Such practices further dampen consumers chance to survive the hard times. Despite receiving billions of dollars of government bailout money, the highest credit card interest rates the banks charge to consumers has never been higher, For example, Bank of America, recipient of $45 billion from the government, charges up to 27.99 percent interest. Citibank, which received $50 billion bailout money, charges up to 29.99 percent. Chase Bank, recipient of $25 billion from the government, charges up to 27.99 percent interest on credit cards. The spread between the highest credit card interest rates and the prime lending rate used to be around 10 percent twenty years ago. Now, the spread has escalated to over 20 percent. While banks are looking for new source of revenue to cover their losses in the home mortgages, high default rates on credit cards have also contributed to the problems. One of the credit card lenders, Advanta Corp., announced they will close all its cardholder's accounts beginning June 1, 2009 to curb its losses.

Swamped by consumer complaints, President Obama and Congress have just passed a Credit Card Reform Act of 2009 to help consumers. Most of the new law will go into effect in July 2010 but some of them will be effective as early as October 2009. Here are highlights of some of the new credit card laws:

1. Restricts Interest Rate Increases:

Prohibit credit card companies from raising interest rate on existing balances or during the first year, unless the account is sixty days behind in making minimum payment, or it is the end of a promised time period for a promotional rate. This does not apply to accounts under variable rates. Promotional rates must be in force for at least six months.

2. Notice of Increase:

After the first year, consumers will have to be notified of any rate increases forty-five days in advance.

3. Fair Application of Payments:

Amounts in excess of the minimum payment must be applied to the highest interest rate balances, except in the last two months before a deferred interest balance is due.

4. Uniform Due Dates:

Due dates will be on the same day of each month and all statements must be mailed at least twenty-one days before payment due date. Card issuers are prohibited from setting early payment deadlines.

5. Set Limits on Fees and Penalties:

If interest rate increased due to minimum payment not received within sixty days, it must be restored to its previous level if minimum payments are made on time for six months. Penalty or late fees must be reasonable and proportional to the omission or violation. No over the limit fee can be imposed unless consumer has asked for it. They will not be allowed to charge late fees if they are late in processing a payment;

6. Prohibit Changing Terms:

Credit card issuers cannot change the terms for repaying a balance, except they may give the consumer either:

(a) Five years to pay off the outstanding balance at the old rate; or

(b) An increased minimum payment but not more than twice as the old minimum payment amount.

There are many other reform provisions that protect young consumers, prevent deceptive marketing of free credit reports, enhanced disclosures and provide gift card protections.

Chapter 21 Short Sale & Short Refinancing

As I discussed in chapter 11, if your LTV is 140 percent or above, your best option is going to be either a short sale or short refinancing. Unless your lender is willing to grant you a huge reduction on principal, loan modification is not going to work because you are so upside down that you may never come out ahead. Your house, which technically is an asset, has become your liability when you have a negative equity. You can choose to walk away and let the bank foreclose on your house which will hurt your credit report more. Short sale or short refinancing will be your better choices if approved by your lender. Most subprime loans, loans started with 90 percent to 100 percent LTV, and those originated during the peak levels of 2005 and 2006 are prime candidates for short sale or short refinancing.

How Does Short Sale Work?

A short sale or short payoff is a great compromise between you and your lender to avoid a foreclosure by selling your house at below the loan payoff amount. In a short sale or short payoff, your lender agrees to accept an amount that is less than what you owe by permitting a sale of your home. To make this work, the transaction requires a qualified buyer to stand by an offer for the duration of the process. Your lender will go through their internal analysis which will focus on two main items:

(1) Your lender will verify your income, recent bank statements, and your assets to make sure you do have a hardship and you truly do not have the money or other resources to continue making the mortgage payments. The purpose of this due diligence is to prevent borrowers walking away from their loan simply because the value dropped below the loan balance. If they have determined you can afford to make payments, they may turn down your short sale and go after you for the deficiency (after foreclosure sale) against your other assets.

(2) They will compare the net proceeds from the short sale to what they project to net from a foreclosure to make sure the short sale is a better option for them. Using the same example shown on chapter 5 under loan modification present value test, assuming the current market value (from a BPO) is $340,000, and your loan balance is $343,700. If your lender forecloses on your home, they will expect to net about $265,200 ($340,000 less 22 percent for selling costs, legal, utilities, maintenance, and distress sale discount, etc.) in about four months. If you present your lender a short sale contract offer of $300,000, less estimated sales expenses of $19,500 (6.5 percent allowance for sales commission, closing costs, etc), your lender will expect to

net about $280,500, closing in about sixty days. Therefore, under this scenario, your lender is better off accepting the short sale offer. Like foreclosure, you will not receive any money from the sale. However, as I will point out later in this chapter, it will not hurt your credit score as much. Even though your lender will come out ahead in this case, that does not mean your lender will automatically accepts the first offer presented to them. Your lender typically will reject the first offer with a counter offer to try pushing the buyer to raise their offer. As long as you know how your lender calculate and work, you have a pretty good idea whether a short sale offer will go through.

What are the Advantages?

Here are some of the advantages of a short sale to the borrower:

1. Once your lender agrees to a short sale, they typically will allow you to stay in the house until it's sold, rent free (you pay only utilities). This will help your cash flow during time of hardship and you could end up staying at your house for several months;
2. Once the house is sold, your credit report will show your mortgage loan as either "paid in full" if your lender sends you a 1099-C for the portion of the debt forgiven, or "settled for less than the amount due", if they do not send you a 1099-C. Either way, it is far better than showing a foreclosure on your credit report. You can then engage a credit repair company (see chapter 30) to help you get the "settled for less" remark removed in a few months.
3. Even if your lender sends you a 1099-C, the amount will be far less than it would have been if your house is foreclosed. In

either case, consult your CPA or refer to chapter 20 to review the IRS's Insolvency Exclusion guidelines for possible exclusion of such debt forgiven amount as income. Almost all lenders will issue you a 1099-C for the forgiven portion of your debt because they have to account for that money gap to balance their books. To do so, they will book the loss portion as money "paid" you, thus they issued you a 1099-C.

4. Since a big chunk of your debt is forgiven, it will allow you to start fresh. Once you recovered from your hardship, you may try to buy back a similar house for, say, 30 percent less.
5. In order to do a short sale, you will have to engage a licensed real estate broker to list your house for sale. You will get the benefit of having the broker handles all matters of the short sale involving your lender and potential buyers, without any cost to you. Unlike loan modification, you will have a consultant on your side at all times at no cost to you. He or she will get paid by your lender but only when the house is sold.
6. There is no out of pocket expense to you. Your lender pays all the expenses and commissions.

Whether it's a foreclosure or a short sale, there is always the potential problem that your lender may seek a "deficiency judgment" against you for the amount they lose. However, almost 99.9 percent of the time, your lender will not want to waste the time and cost to seek for a deficiency judgment because you probably can't pay it anyway. In all likelihood, your lender will send you a 1099-C and close the file. Once they sent you a 1099-C, they cannot seek a deficiency judgment. They can only do one or the other, not both.

Debt Forgiveness Tax Relief

Congress passed a H.R. 3648 Bill in October 2007 – a Mortgage Forgiveness Debt Relief Act of 2007, which became law on December 20, 2007. It amends the IRS Code to exclude from gross income (non-taxable) amounts attributable to discharge (debt forgiven), prior to January 1, 2010, of indebtedness incurred to acquire a principal residence (mortgage loan for the purchase of your primary home). It limits to $2 million the excludable amount of such indebtedness and reduces the basis of a principal residence by the amount of discharged indebtedness excluded from income. It sets forth rules for determining the allowable amount of the exclusion for taxpayers with non-qualifying indebtedness and taxpayers who are insolvent.

Among other provisions, it also allows a surviving spouse to exclude from gross income up to $500,000 of the gain from the sale or exchange of a principal residence owned jointly with a deceased spouse if the sale or exchange occurs within two years of the death of the spouse and other ownership and use requirements have been met.

The government realized that due to the drastic reduction in home values, a great number of troubled borrowers do not qualify for loan modification or refinancing. As a result, the government unveiled the Foreclosure Alternative Program, providing incentives to all parties working together on short sales. Please see chapter 13 for more details.

What is Short Refinancing?

A short refinancing is like a combination of a refinancing and a short sale. In this case, you are refinancing your own loan with a new loan that is less than the amount needed to pay off the existing loan. In order to do that, your existing lender must approve it like a short sale. The new lender will simply treat you as a new borrower and you must meet all the requirement of a refinancing I discussed in chapter 12 and 13. The benefit here is that, since the new loan amount is reduced by the deficiency of the short sale, the lower payment may help you qualify. Also, unlike short sales, you don't have to wait to find a buyer for your house. You are the "new" buyer". Overall, short sales are far more popular and straight forward than short refinancing.

Short Sale Process – Step-by-Step

Short sale is a very time consuming process and most buyers do not have the patience to wait six to ten weeks, sometimes much longer, for a lender's decision after an offer is submitted. It will speed up the process if you are fully prepared in advance. Let me walk you through the typical process:

1. Engage a real estate broker who has experience in dealing with short sales. Advise your broker you will be doing a short sale. Many states now have a "Short Sale Listing Addendum" which authorized the broker to contact your lender regarding approving a short sale and to advertise your home as a short sale, as well as advising you regarding possible tax, credit and other legal consequences, other alternatives to a short sale, and how short sale works.
2. Determining the listing price. The success of a short sale lies almost solely on what is the current market value of your house. Ask your broker to do a BPO caters to a short sale (lean towards the low end of the range – see chapter 10). Whether your lender accepts or rejects an offer will depends on the offer's deviation form the current market value. Your lender will want

to sell your house as high as possible but they also know they cannot sell higher than the market value. Therefore, typically they will consider any offer not more than 10 percent below the current market value. As a rule of thumb, the first lien lender would discount the BPO value by 5 percent to 10 percent, and the second lien holder would discount it by 25 percent.

3. If the house is in need of repairs, make a list of the repairs and get an estimate (using estimates on the high side will help you more). You can then deduct the estimated repairs from the BPO value.

4. Gather all your mortgage statements together to determine how upside down are you? If the current market value less selling costs falls below 50 percent of your outstanding debts, you have virtually no chance of getting a short sale approved. In most cases, lenders settle for short sales about 20 percent to 30 percent below the loan payoff. Lenders based their decision on their internal "Acceptable Loss Severity" and their "Return-on-Investment" analysis. Typically, Acceptable Loss Severity for most lenders are:
   (a) First lien lender: 20 percent
   (b) Second lien lender: 95 percent to 99 percent
   (c) Second lien Home Equity Line of Credit (HELOC): 80 percent

These are the typical internal allowance for losses by lenders after all closing costs and sales commissions are deducted. Higher losses may be allowed as long as the offer is within 10 percent of the current market value. If your current market value is less than 20 percent below your loan balances, you may only need to negotiate a short sale with your second lien lender. First lien lender generally is not willing to allow any money going to the second lien lender. As a gesture to make a short sale work, however, they sometimes agree to give them a token money from $1,000 to $5,000. This is not because they are being nice, but they know they will lose more money in a foreclosure and the second lien lender is not going cooperate and agree to a short sale getting nothing out of it. If the second lien lender does not approve the short sale, the property will end up in foreclosure. Thus, a second lien lender is willing to lose 95 percent to 99 percent of their loan in a short sale. HELOC (see chapter 12) lenders generally will allow losses up to 80 percent. If they are getting very little money offered by the first lien lender, you may offer a compromise asking the second lien lender to give you a small unsecured loan to make up the difference so they will not hold up your short sale.

5. The only figure your first lien lender cares is the bottom line figure on the HUD or closing statement. They want to compare the net amount they will receive from a short sale to an estimated net amount they will receive if they foreclosure and sell the house as an REO or at an auction. Therefore, in order for the lender to approve a short sale, they must be convinced that they will lose more money if foreclosed. Fortunately, in most cases, short sale will bring the lender more money. This is because:
   (a) A short sale will close almost immediately since an offer is already on the table while a foreclosure will take at least four months to process. After that, they still have to locate a buyer.
   (b) Short sale offers generally are more in line with the current market value while people will almost never pay full market value on a foreclosure.
   (c) Foreclosure will involve more legal fees and holding costs, not to mention possible vandalism in empty homes. In the case of short sale, most homeowners will stay in the house, paying utilities, and keep the house maintained.

6. To be prepared, your broker should open title at a title insurance company the moment you signed the listing agreement. He should then order a preliminary title report which will show all the liens on your property and any unpaid taxes or HOA dues. All liens must be paid off or negotiated a release before you can sell your house. This report will enable your broker to know each party he may have to negotiate a short sale. Your broker should further ask the title company to order a payoff amount from each lender. Once you have all the payoff figures before reduction, and all the closing costs and taxes to be paid out of closing, then you know what amount the house has to sell in order to break even. Then using the BPO figure as a guideline, you can estimate how upside down are you.
7. Once you have all that, your broker should get a head start by contacting your lender(s) to start the short sale process without an offer. Lenders require a short sale package to be approved in addition to approving a sale. Therefore, you can save a lot of time if your lender will first approve your short sale package ahead of receiving any offers. Sometime, your may even get a "pre-approved" short sale amount. However, most lenders do not set any pre-approved amount become it may soon becomes obsolete with today's fast changing financial environment. In any case, your broker should still notify your lender that he is engaged to do a short sale for you. This is particularly important if you are already behind in your payments and you want your lender know that you are working with a broker on a short sale so that they will not continue with the foreclosure proceedings or harass you from their collection department.
8. Once an offer is received, the title company will be able to prepare a HUD statement using the offering price so you can present it to your lender with an exact net figure for their

approval. Your lender will then be able to determine if the offer is acceptable. If not, they will come back telling you the offer is too low.

9. Before your lender will even consider a short sale offer, you must present your lender the Short Sale Package as follows:
   (a) Your lender's specific short sale forms
   (b) Borrowers information
   (c) Borrower's authorization and Release form to your broker
   (d) Most recent mortgage statements
   (e) Hardship letter
   (f) Financial statement
   (g) Last two years tax returns
   (h) Most recent two months bank statements
   (i) Last two months pay stubs
   (j) BPO
   (k) Cost of Repairs
   (l) Listing Agreement
   (m) Sales contract if you already have an offer
   (n) Estimated HUD – if you already have an offer

Even if everything is done correctly, processing a short sale is still going to be difficult and time consuming, particularly if there is more than one lien. You may run into a situation whereby the second or third lien holder, or a mechanic's lien holder, may hold up everyone by demanding more money. Even though in a foreclosure sale, there may not be anything left after paying the first lien holder, this does not mean they will sign a release and walk away with nothing. As a rule of thumb, the more liens on your home, the less chance you will succeed in a short sale.

If you need both the first and second lien lenders taking a loss in order to make a sale, then you should first approach the first lien lenders Under such a scenario, it is almost certain that the second mortgage holder will be lucky to get $5,000. The first lien lender usually rejects an initial offer saying they cannot accept it because it's too low. Even if the offer will result in a bottom figure well within their 20 percent Acceptable Loss Severity, the negotiator will still want to get as high a figure as he can get. They want to see if the buyer is willing to raise their offer before taking them seriously. Some major banks offer extra bonus to a negotiator who is able to close a deal resulting in a higher recovery percentage (i.e. lower loss severity). Your broker will have to work hard to convince the negotiator the offer on the table is at or near the current market value. Most short sale, even after you receive an offer from a buyer, will take at least six to ten weeks to process through the negotiation with all the lien holders. Overall, from the time you engaged the broker, the whole process will take an average of four to six months. This is why you rely on your broker to do the works for you. Buy your broker a nice dinner if he is able to pull your short sale through all parties.

As difficult as it may take, once the short sale is concluded, all parties win:

1. You get out of a jam and, most likely, your credit report will only show the debt as "paid in full".
2. Your lender gets more money recovered as compared to foreclosure.
3. Your broker gets paid a commission at a time home sales are slow.
4. The buyer managed to buy your house at a super discount

Chapter 22 Hardship Letter for Short Sale

As I discussed in hardship letter for loan modification (see chapter 14), all lenders require a hardship letter before they will process your short sale request. Again, this is just a requirement they have to follow. The loss mitigator really does not care about the details of your hardship so keep your letter simple. All the valid hardship reasons listed in chapter 14 is applicable here. What is not considered a valid hardship reason, despite the obvious, is to tell your lender you want a short sale because there is no equity in the house due to market value dropped. This is because your lender does not want a borrower who has resources to make existing payment to get away with a short sale just to avoid losing money on the house. After all, if the short sale will not hurt his credit report, wouldn't it be a good business sense passing the loss to your lender? That's why your lender wants to see your tax returns, bank statements and financial statement to see if you indeed have the capability of making existing loan payments.

Is Hardship Letter Different from Loan Modification?

One significant difference between a hardship letter for loan modification and a short sale is that, in a short sale letter, you do not need to state how you are planning to get out of the trouble because you are selling your house.

The key elements of your hardship letter for a short sale are:

1. Describe the hardship that caused you to be unable to make the existing mortgage payment.
2. You do not have the income to qualify for a loan modification or refinancing.
3. You have no choice but to leave the house, but you don't want to file bankruptcy.

Sample Hardship Letter # 1

Date

Names

Address

Loan Number

To Whom It May Concern:

Due to the loss of my job (or whatever is your hardship reasons), I am unable to continue making mortgage payment on my house. I have tried all efforts to find a new job but it does not appear my financial difficulties will improve any time soon. Therefore, I regret to inform you that I have no choice but to give up my home. I do not want to file for bankruptcy but I do sincerely hope you will help me on a short sale instead of a foreclosure.

Your assistance in this matter will be greatly appreciated.

Sincerely,

Your Signature

Printed name

(I suggest you handwrite your letter and keep it simple)

Sample Hardship Letter #2

Date

Names & Address

Loan Number

To Whom It May Concern:

I have been working with your loss mitigation department on the above referenced loan for a possible short sale situation. Based on the BPO by my broker, the current fair market value of my home is about $340,000, while my loan balance is $353,570. Having received zero offers for four months, I am pleased to present you a contract offer for a price of $315,000 (93 percent of fair market value). I understand this offer will net you only about $295,000 after deducting sales expenses, but I believe it is the highest offer you can reasonably expect in today's distress market for this home. According to my broker's assessment, if you reject this reasonable offer and end up foreclosing on my home, you will probably net less than $270,000 on a REO sale. I do not assume to be able to dictate your calculations but, all things considered, it appears if you can recover 83.4 percent of the loan amount and close within sixty days, you will not want to lose this short sale opportunity.

Time is of essence so your early response to this offer will be greatly appreciated

Sincerely,
Your Signature
Printed name

Enclosures

Chapter 23 Short Sale with Buy Back Option

In this scenario, you can sell the home to an investor at a discounted price agreed by your lender (Short Sale), and retain an option to lease and possibly buy it back from the investor at a later date.

How Short Sale with Lease Option Buy Back Works?

This is an excellent option if you cannot make your mortgage payment even with a modified payment but really love your home so much that you will do everything you can to stay in your home. Since there are a lot of bargain investors looking to buy foreclosed or short sale houses and they will like to lease out the house to get some income, such an arrangement could benefit all parties. The investor will have to agree to let you lease the house back at a rental rate far lower than your existing mortgage payment. The option to purchase back the house will be much higher than what the investor is paying to buy the house because he is doing it with the intention to profit when the market value goes back up. While all this sounds great, it is not practical to expect such a deal can be structured when you are dealing with:

(1) Your lender who wants the best and highest offer open to all buyers

(2) Your real estate broker is obligated to submit all offer to the lender

(3) Your investor has to be the highest bidder before entering into any side agreement with you. Typically, this type of deals are done through an investor found by you shortly before the foreclosure and you ask your real estate broker to handle the transaction and obtain an agreement from your lender's loss mitigation department to agree to the deal prior to the foreclosure sale.

Chapter 24: Reverse Mortgage

For senior citizens who are sixty-two or over and is having difficulties to make their mortgage payments, their best choice may be obtaining a reverse mortgage. Refinancing with a reverse mortgage is kind of like taking out a series of home equity loans. You do not have to make any payments. All payments, principal and interest, are added on to your loan balance every month so you will owe more and more. In fact, you can even take money out in one limp sum, a line of credit, or even like a monthly payment to you. Thus, it is called "reverse" mortgage because it could be structures to pay you monthly. Needless to say, all money comes out of your home equity and added onto your loan. Nevertheless, it will help your cash flow at a time and age that your income may be reducing or not coming at all. Without any positive cash flow, you will not be qualified for refinancing or loan modification.

Who Qualifies for a Reverse Mortgage?

There are a lot of regulations and restrictions for a reverse mortgage:

1. You must be at least sixty-two years old.
2. The property must be your primary residence.
3. The existing mortgage must be paid off from the new reverse mortgage loan like a refinancing.
4. Many lenders require the borrower to receive counseling by a HUD-approved counselor or you may select from a list of approved agencies. They want to make sure you understand the loan program entirely before living off the equity of your home.
5. About 90 percent of all reverse mortgages are FHA reverse mortgages. The amount of money available to the senior is based on the lesser of the appraised value of the home or the county limit. Most counties in the nation have a limit of $417,000. These loans are insured by the government and the lender is not at risk.
6. The loan is due on sale or is no longer occupied as your primary residence. In the case of more than one borrower, repayment is triggered when the last borrower permanently moves out.

How Does Reverse Mortgage Work?

A reverse mortgage is a "non-recourse" loan, which means you, your heirs, or your estate cannot be held liable to repay more than the appraised value of the home at the maturity of the loan. If the loan balance plus all accrued interest and fees exceeds the value of the home, you, your heirs, or your estate will only be obligated to repay an amount up to the current appraised value of the property. As long as the borrower, or the last of more than one borrower, still lives in the home, you do not have to make any monthly mortgage payments to the lender. Interest on reverse mortgages is typically based on variable rates, although some lenders now offer fixed rate as well. Interest is accrued on your loan. You can deduct the interest expenses on your income tax return when the loan is repaid. Funds received from a reverse mortgage are generally categorized as loan advances and not taxable income.

Most importantly, qualifications for reverse mortgages rely almost solely on whether you have enough equity in your house. There is no minimum credit score requirement and even bad credit history will not matter. There is no minimum ownership time requirement. As long as you (sixty-two or over) own and live in the house at the time of the loan, you are qualified. The amount of money you can take, however, depends on the equity and age of the borrower. Generally speaking, the older the person, the more money you can take out simply because the lender thinks you will die sooner, thus, the loan will be paid off sooner. There is no payment of principal or interest for the rest of the borrower's life. Title of the property stays with the borrower. The lender holds a lien on the property just like any other mortgage loans. This is a program designed by the deferral government and incurred by the Federal Housing Authority to help senior citizens who cannot survive solely on social security benefits alone.

Chapter 25 Forensic Loan Doc Audit

Forensic Loan Doc Audit is conducted by an attorney to review all your loan documents looking for mistakes and violations. According to one law firm that engaged in a lot of such loan audits, over 90 percent of ARM or Option ARM loans contains some federal violations.

What are the Common Mistakes the Lenders Make?

Here are some of the common mistakes made by lenders on loan documents or closing paper works.

1. Truth in Lending Violations
2. Fraudulent activities
3. Under disclosure
4. Misrepresentation
5. Over charge on HUD
6. APR is higher than originally disclosed

7. Predatory lending

Basically, violations of your legal rights give you negotiating power. In some extreme cases of violation and if raised within three years, you could potentially rescind entire loan and demand your lender to refund every bit of money you paid. In practicality, however, most violations are small such as APR is 0.125 percent higher than originally disclosed, or the HUD shows a $35 overcharge. Nevertheless, any mistake could give you some bargaining or negotiating power, or to speed up the process, whether you try to stop a foreclosure or requesting a loan modification or a short sale. Typically, this is used as your last resort before foreclosure. Most attorneys charge $250 to $500 for this service.

What Documents Needed for an Audit?

If you want to conduct such an audit, your attorney will need all of the following documents:

1. Final signed HUD closing statement
2. Estimated closing statement
3. Promissory Note, including riders and addendums
4. Truth-ion-Lending Statement
5. Itemization of amount financed
6. Good Faith Estimate (GFE) – include all provided you
7. Notice of Right to Cancel (if refinance)
8. Loan Application (1003)
9. Initial Loan Disclosures provided by broker and/or lender
10. Most recent copies of mortgage statements
11. Lender's instructions

12. ARM disclosures
13. Any and all documents and correspondence you have from your loan package or from your lender.

Chapter 26 Deed-In-Lieu of Foreclosure

A Deed-in-Lieu of Foreclosure is to allow the home to be conveyed or deeded back to the mortgage lender, preventing the lengthy and negative foreclosure process. If you cannot sell your home, cannot afford to pay the mortgage, no income to qualify for refinancing, loan modification or short sale, then all that is left is waiting for the house to be foreclosed. If so, a better option that may be available for you than foreclosure is to sign (with notary) the ownership of the house back to your lender, using a simple Deed-in-Lieu of Foreclosure form which is another form of deed. Once the lender recorded the signed Deed-in-Lieu of Foreclosure, your lender will take possession of your house. It's simple, quick and instant. Your lender will save a lot of time and cost to prevent the foreclosure process. To qualify, the property must be vacant, have no other liens or judgments against it, and has been unable to sell at current fair market value for more than ninety days. Otherwise, the only way to clear up other liens is for your first lien lender to foreclose and wipe all junior liens. Not all states allow the Deed-in-lieu program.

What are Your Benefits of Deed-in-Lieu of Foreclosure?

Here are some of the benefits of Deed-in-Lieu of Foreclosure:

1. It will release you from all debts associated with the mortgage and stop your payment obligation immediately, including property taxes, insurance, etc. payments;
2. Once accepted, you will not be pursued for any loss associated with this transaction;
3. The credit agencies will report the account as "voluntary repossession" rather than foreclosure.

What Documents Do You Need to Prepare?

If this is the route you choose to take, then your lender will need the following, which is very similar to the short sale requirements:

1. Hardship letter, similar to the short sale hardship letter
2. Pay check stubs – two most current stubs from each borrower
3. Tax returns for last two years
4. Bank statements for the most recent two months
5. Completed Financial Evaluation form provided by your lender
6. Property Preservation Authorization form provided by your lender

In this scenario, there is not much for your lender to decide. You are basically walking away from the house and it is to their advantage to take over the house instantly than to spend time and money on a foreclosure. Unless the Financial Evaluation shows you own a lot of assets that they may go after your personal guarantee, in most cases, they will simply accept your Deed-in-Lieu of Foreclosure.

The government's new Foreclosure Alternative Program also provides incentives on Deed-in-Lieu of Foreclosures if the short sale option does not work on some borrowers. Please see chapter 13 for more details.

Chapter 27 Foreclosure Process - Mortgagee

This is probably the worst case scenario aside from filing for bankruptcy. Not only you will lose your home, against your wishes, you will also seriously impact your credit report for seven years. According to Fannie Mae's guidelines, you will have to wait at least four years after the completion of a foreclosure. Even after seven years, it could still affect your chance of obtain a loan because all loan applications ask you whether you have ever been foreclosed upon. Foreclosure is a legal process in which your home (or other real properties) is sold to satisfy your mortgage debt for which your home was pledged as collateral. Foreclosure can also occur if you have unpaid real property tax liens, federal tax liens and, to some limitations, a homeowners association dues liens (see chapter 28).

Foreclosure Process – Step-by-Step

Here is the foreclosure process; some state laws may vary:

1. When you are thirty days late in your payment, your lender will typically send you reminder and warning letters urging you to make the payment.
2. When you get past sixty days late (some lenders may give you more time), an official Notice of Default will be filed with your county's office.
3. Shortly thereafter, usually within ten business days, the Notice of Default is mailed to you by the Trustee holding your mortgage. You will be given a thirty days time to cure your default (or whatever statutory period of days).
4. If the default is not cured within the thirty days, another Notice of Default will be mailed to you. It is up to your lender how much time they want to give you for the Notice of Default period. The actual foreclosure procedure does not begin until your lenders feels they have exhausted all avenues for curing the payment delinquency. During such time, your lender will probably contact you several times, by mail or by phone, prior to beginning the foreclosure process. This is your last chance to initiate any of the other options I discussed in this book. Any of the other options is better than a foreclosure.
5. When your lender determined that the Notice of Default period ended and there is no other alternatives but to proceed with the foreclosure (this will likely occur about ninety days after the initial Notice of Default was sent to you), then they will send you a Notice of Trustee Sale (NOTS) by certified mail. Although each county may have its own set of rules, typically, NOTS must be posted on the property and at the county court

house (or published in newspaper) at least twenty-one days prior to the Auction Sale Date. In many states, all foreclosure sales must be carried out on a pre-determined date of each month set by the county, such as the second Tuesday of the month.

6. NOTS is recorded in your county's recorder's office at least fourteen days prior to the Sale Date.
7. Your final right to reinstate expires five days prior to the Sale Date.
8. On the day of the Trustee Sale, The property is sold to the highest bidder or reverts back to the lender as a REO (Real Estate Owned – bank owned) property. The lender typically bid at the defaulted debt amount plus foreclosure costs. If a third party bids higher, the lender will get fully paid for the debt and recovers all the costs.
9. By law, if the property is sold higher than the debt owed plus foreclosure costs, the surplus amount must be refunded to the borrower who lost title to the property. However, bargain hunters bid at foreclosure auctions typically will not pay too much more than the lender's bid unless there are multiple parties bidding. Properties at foreclosure auctions are sold "as-is" for cash without any warranties.

Chapter 28 Foreclosure – Tax Liens

Mortgage foreclosure by your lender is not the only type of foreclosures that can take your house. Here are some other possibilities:

Property Tax Lien Foreclosures

Real Property Tax liens – real property, such as your house, is subject to taxation by your state, county, city, school district, municipal utilities district, public improvement district, tax increment reinvestment zone, or any other district or corporation given power by the legislature to levy real property tax. The tax liability is a lien against the taxed property. The tax entity typically gives you about six months with penalties to pay your delinquent property taxes. After six months, penalties and interest will escalate and your account will be turned over to an attorney for collection. At some point, usually after one to two years depends on each taxing entity, they will start the foreclosure proceeding through civil litigation. Most states will not allow non-judicial foreclosure. I advise you to consult with an attorney on your legal rights. The problem is, there is very little you can defend yourselves in such a lawsuit. In some states, like Texas, the taxpayer has the right to redeem his property at any time during the next two years by paying the auction buyer double what was paid for the property at the foreclosure sale. Therefore, the buyer at the auction sale does not get immediate clear title. After the two-year redemption period expires, the taxing entity may resell the property with good and clear title.

Federal Tax Lien Foreclosures

Whenever you have any delinquent federal taxes, the Internal Revenue Service may proceed to assess the delinquent taxes against the taxpayer and place a lien upon the taxpayer's property like a judgment lien. Like the judgment lien (or Mechanic's lien on your property), you will not be able to sell your property unless these liens are released. The IRS has the right to foreclose its lien by a non-judicial seizure and sale of the property except your homestead. Under present law, the IRS must give notice of intent to seize taxpayer property thirty days before seizure. In general, the IRS may not seize your homestead property unless the collection of the tax is in jeopardy or the IRS district director or assistant director approves in writing. The buyers at the IRS foreclosure sale buy the property subject to all liens senior to the IRS lien.

Can Homeowners Association Foreclose Your Home?

This is by far the most controversy of all lien holders who have the right to foreclose on a property. Not all states or counties allow the HOA to foreclose on a home just because they fail to pay HOA dues. However, many states or counties do permit such foreclosure sale but have set strict requirements of notices and redemption period to protect homeowners. Again, I advise every reader caught in such a situation to consult an attorney to clarify your legal rights.

Can Judgment Liens Go After Your Home?

In the case of a judgment lien, many states allow you to sell your homestead house by giving the lien holder a thirty day notice of your homestead and your intention to record a release of judgment lien due to homestead. However, the holder of the judgment lien has the legal right to garnish your bank accounts if it has your name on the account. Therefore, when your homestead home is sold, and you deposited the sales proceeds into your bank account, the judgment lien holder can take the money out of your bank account without your notice because the sales proceed is no longer protected by homestead. Some lenders will notify you and allow you to challenge the garnishment in court.

How to Avoid Tax Loan Schemes?

Homeowners short of money to pay mortgages quite frequently also have problem paying their property taxes. You may receive tons of solicitations to give your tax loans to help you out. This could be potentially devastating. These kinds of "loan sharks" not only charge you with high interest rates, they also make you assign the tax lien rights to them. This means, if you default in their loan, they will step in to replace your tax entity and foreclose on your home. This is dangerous because these lenders have every intention to take over your property and they will grab the opportunity the moment you default. Your tax entity, on the other hand, typically will give you a very long time before any foreclosure proceedings, not to mention the redemption period. Also, you may be able to negotiate with your tax entity for a payment plan if you are in a hardship.

Chapter 29 Bankruptcy

Whether or not to file a bankruptcy petition is probably the most important decision you have to make, and the decision is rarely simple. Each person or family has a unique situation, and most states have different bankruptcy laws as far as what constitute as protected or exempted properties. Naturally, it is wrong not to pay your debts, and creditors will get very upset if you choose to go this route to get away from paying them. Having said that, the law is the law, and as long as you abide by the law, it is possible that you could have a fresh start from financial mistakes you made. Perhaps our forefather had taken a page from the Bible and enacted into a law:

> "At the end of every seven years, you must cancel debts. This is how it is to be done: Every creditor shall cancel the loan he has made to his fellow Israelite. He shall not require payment from his fellow Israelite or brother, because the Lord's time for canceling debts has been proclaimed."
> Deuteronomy 15: 1-2)

Chapter 13 bankruptcy filing will remain on your credit report for seven years, even if it is dismissed. In this chapter, I will give you a glimpse of the highlight but you should definitely consult a bankruptcy attorney and, by law, you are required to take credit counseling courses within one hundred and eighty days of filing. The principal goal of bankruptcies is to have most unsecured debts discharged. It is possible that filing bankruptcy can liquidate your debts, place an automatic stay on lawsuits, and/or allow more time before a foreclosure of your home can take place.

The three basic forms of voluntary bankruptcy filings are:

Chapter 13 Bankruptcy

This is for individuals with regular income doing a payment plan to spread out payments of his debts and get some instant relief. This is also called a Wages Earner Plan. People with income above their state's median income who can pay at least $6,000 over five years ($100 per month) would be forced by the bankruptcy court to file under chapter 13. Under the latest amendment of the law in 2005, people can no longer choose to file chapter 7 freely to erase their debts entirely. The change was aimed at prevent people from running up their credit cards debts to the limit and then file a chapter 7 bankruptcy to erase them. Under chapter 13, you will be required to prepare a budget and to determine a fixed amount each month to be tendered to the court towards the payment plan of the debts listed on your schedule. Over a period of three to five years, when all payments are made to satisfy the creditors, your bankruptcy will be dismissed. Besides regular income requirement, to be eligible to file chapter 13 bankruptcy, you cannot have more than $100,000 of non-contingent, liquidated, unsecured debts or more than $350,000 of non-contingent, liquidated, secured debts. There are other limitations if you have filed bankruptcy previously. The payment plan must be approved by the creditors and the court.

Chapter 7 Bankruptcy

This is a total liquidation plan for either individuals or businesses. Under chapter 7, you or the business will surrender all your assets to the court (other than those protected under homestead). The trustee will liquidate all the unprotected assets, except secured creditor will take the secured assets. After deducting legal, court and trustee fees, all remaining funds will be distributed to unsecured creditors proportionally. chapter 7 filings will stay on your credit report for ten

Chapter 11 is a reorganization plan for businesses, which is not covered by this personal guidebook.

What is Considered Fraudulent Transfer?

It is important that you provide a full disclosure of all your assets to the court. If not, you may be committing a bankruptcy fraud. Most importantly, it is illegal to transfer any assets to your family members or related "insider" parties within the twelve months preceding the bankruptcy filing ("fraudulent conveyance"). The federal bankruptcy trustee, assigned by the court, will investigate all your payments, bank statements, or other non-cash transfers in the past twelve months. If any fraudulent transfer or fraudulent conveyance is found, those recipients will be under a court order to return them to the bankruptcy estate. In addition, any transfers of assets, properties or payments made within ninety days prior to the bankruptcy filing to any unrelated party may be subject to be reviewed. Even though those are payments or transfers made to un-related parties, they may be considered a "preference transfer". If those people or entities received 100% payment of their debts while other creditors end up getting only 70 percent of what they were owed, then a preference treatment has occurred. The court wants to prevent a debtor from giving away property or money to shield it from creditors, or one or more unsecured creditors are favored over others.

Many homeowners choose to file a chapter 13 bankruptcy to stop the foreclosure of their home. They will then use the chapter 13 payment plan to include making regular mortgage payment in the future and the delinquent amount spread over three to five years. This is possible if they can afford to continue making future mortgage payment. In the case of chapter 7, however, the bankruptcy filing will only delay the foreclosure proceeding. Once the bankruptcy court assigns a trustee, your lender will petition to the trust for permission to proceed with foreclosure if they are holding a valid first lien on your home.

What Assets are protected or exempt from Creditors?

Your home, if it's your homestead, may be protected against other creditors except those holding a lien on your home. In states like Texas, Florida, Iowa, Kansas, South Dakata, you homestead home is fully protected and exempt without limitation, even if it's a $10 million mansion if they are purchased more than forty months prior to your bankruptcy filing. If purchased within forty months, only $125,000 is exempted. In the other states, the exemption varies. For example, in Massachusetts, you can exempt $500,000 worth of equity in your homestead estate; in California, you can exempt up to $150,000; in

New York, up to $50,000. Therefore, any net proceeds after selling your home and paying off your mortgage, less the exempted amount, will not be protected from unsecured creditors. In addition to homestead, you can protect a very small amount of allowance for a car, household goods, furniture, etc. You may also choose to go by the federal bankruptcy law instead of your state bankruptcy law. Due to the variations between states, I urge you to rely solely on the advice of your bankruptcy attorney or a credit counselor.

By simply filing a bankruptcy petition, all civil lawsuits against you will be brought to an abrupt halt. The automatic stay freezes your assets as of the date of bankruptcy filing, preventing creditors from collecting from a lawsuit or a judgment, and stops all collection effort. The stay can be lifted by the court at any time but, in the case of chapter 13 filing, it could last for the duration of your three to five year payment plan.

Sometimes, you may get lucky and get away with some of your debts totally clean and legal. In one case study, a person was involved in a lawsuit that could cost him a large sum of money. Even though he was innocent, he didn't' have the enormous money needed to defend the lawsuit. Thus, at the advice of his attorney, he filed for a chapter 13 bankruptcy to force an immediate stay of the lawsuit. After several months, the lawsuit was settled out of court and the bankruptcy was dismissed. Something interesting occurred. At the time he filed for bankruptcy, he had several credit card debts totaling about $35,000. Shortly after his filing, the credit card companies deem the debts uncollectible and sold them to collection agencies pennies on the dollar. The collection agencies tried to harass him for the debt but were forced to stop with the automatic stay. Later the collection agencies gave up and wrote off those debts. After the bankruptcy dismissed, the person's credit report showed those credit cards with a zero balance owed. He has since recovered from his problems and his credit score restored back to over 800, despite a bankruptcy continues to show on his credit report. Therefore, nothing is cut and dry. Every person's situation is different. I advise you to learn and decide what is best for you.

A married couple does not have to both file for bankruptcy. You can have one of the two to file for bankruptcy so only one person' credit report will show the filing. If debts are owed by both persons, it may be preferable to file bankruptcy jointly to avoid creditors going after the non-filing spouse. The same filing fee can be applied to one or both of the same family.

Finally, even if you do not want to file for bankruptcy, you could be forced into a bankruptcy by your creditors. This is called Involuntary Bankruptcy Filing. There are a number of restrictions that the creditors must abide.

Chapter 30 Credit Repair

Once you have gone through the debt settlement program and get all your debts settled, then you may want to consider whether to engage a credit repair company to try removing some of the negative items from your credit report.

Does Credit Repair Really Work?

A credit repair company is completely different from a debt settlement company. A credit repair company files disputes with the credit reporting agencies repeatedly based on loopholes in federal law over six to twelve months. They may be able to help you remove less serious remarks such as "settled in full" or "settled in reduced amount" but the more serious items, such as bankruptcies or judgments are almost impossible to get them removed with some court releases. Even if they are successful in removing certain adverse items from your credit report, chances are they are only temporary removed pending investigation. Once they are re-verified, those items will re-appear on your credit report. In general, unless an item on your credit report is listed in error, the debt settlement companies will probably unable to get them removed.

Be aware of a credit repair scam called "file Segregation". File segregation promises a chance to hide unfavorable credit information by creating a new entity. This may sound great to solve your credit report problems, but file segregation is illegal and you could end up in jail.

Fees charged by these companies varies, depends on how many and how serious are the items you intend to remove. Many will charge you a fee from $1,000 to $2,000. There is no guarantee they will be successful but if you do not mind to pay the fee hoping for a small chance of getting some of the adverse items removed from your credit report, then there is no hard to try.

Chapter 31 Credit Reports, Credit Scores

Our credit industry relies heavily on consumer's credit reports and credit scores to determine whether a person is credit worthy. The most common credit scoring system was developed by the Fair Isaac Corporation which is known as FICO score. It is used by major credit bureaus to evaluate your credit history. The system considers factors like how many credit cards you have and how quickly you pay your bills, and assigns you a rating between 300 and 850.

The Flaws in the Credit System

The system is not perfect and based on the subprime disaster, it is obvious that major changes will be needed. The way the system is set up now, a rich person with lots of assets and no debts may not be able to obtain a simple loan while a college grad with no assets, owed one car payment and a couple of credit cards could have a higher credit score and no problem getting any loan. This is because the rich person paid cash for his house and his car, and he pays his single American

Express card in full each month, leaving no carry forward balances. His credit report will show "lack of payment history" because there are virtually no creditors reporting his payment pattern. His credit score is likely to be just an average figure. In comparison, the college grad barely making his car loan payment, and leaving some balances on a couple of his four credit cards would have a clean and good credit report, showing all payments on time and a low debt ratio. His credit score may be around 720. With a higher credit score, you can even get lower insurance premiums because insurance companies consider people with better money management at lower risk. You may question the logic behind this because you often see rich people drive fast sports cars which, appears to be more risky.

In order to cure some of the problems, Beacon Mortgage Score from Equifax launched a new FICO industry score in April 2009, specifically designed to help mortgage lenders make the best possible risk decisions. The new scoring model assesses fifteen additional score reason codes using data variables derived from Equifax consumer files, selected specifically to predict mortgage repayment risk. Early tests suggest that the use of the new scoring system identified up to 25 percent more of the high-risk mortgages and home equity lines-of-credit that later became seriously delinquent. Lenders are also considering changes to the formula that is used to determine the "credit worthiness" of borrowers. Some of the proposed changes to the scoring system include:

1. Stronger penalties for late payments
2. Better rewards for prompt payment
3. Different types of debt will be scored differently.

Credit Reporting Bureaus

Until the system is fixed, we all have to live by the current system and figure out what you can do to maximize your credit score. Higher credit score will enable you to obtain loans with higher limits, lower interest rates, and lower down payment if you are buying a home. Due to the high identity theft going around, it is essential that you check your own credit reports regularly, or at least once every six months. Someone may have stolen your identity and applied for credits in your name and ruin your credit report without your awareness. By law you are entitled to one free credit report per year. In addition, if you are denied credit, insurance or employment within the past sixty days, or if you believe you are a victim of fraud, you are entitled to a free report. Most "free" credit reports do not give you your credit score which you have to pay a small fee to obtain. There are many companies offer credit reports on Web sites that advertise "free". However, in most cases, you will end up having to pay at the end. Go to government sponsored site www.AnnualCreditReport.com to get a truly free credit report but no one provides credit score free. Many companies offer 3-in-1 credit reports/scores at a discount. If you find any mistake on your credit report, you can dispute it to each of the three major credit reporting agencies or credit bureaus. They will conduct an investigation and remove it within thirty days if appropriate.

Here are the three major credit bureaus:

1. Equifax Credit Information Services
   P. O. Box 740241, Atlanta, GA 30374-0241
   www.equifax.com 800-685-1111

2. Experian
   P. O. Box 9701, Allen, TX 75013
   www.experian.com 888-397-3742

3. TransUnion Consumer Solutions
   P. O. Box 2000, Chester, PA 19022-2000
   www.tuc.com 800-888-4213

What is in a Credit Report?

Your credit report will show all of the following:

1. Creditor's name, address, SS #, last employment, DOB
2. Account number
3. Type of account – Revolving, Installment, Mortgage, Line-of-Credit, Open Loan
4. Date account was open
5. Credit line
6. High Credit - highest amount ever charged
7. Current balance – as of the date of the report
8. Last activities – last activities month/year or last delinquent month/year
9. Duration - # of installments (promissory note term, amortization)
10. Frequency of each payment
11. Monthly payment amount
12. Months Reviewed – Total number of months reviewed
13. Each month in the entire history of the account, one of the following will show: no history, account in good standing, 30-59 days late, 60-89 days late, 90-119 days late, 120-149 days, late 150-179 days late, 180+ days late, collection, foreclosure, voluntary surrender, repossession, charge off.

14. Last Payment amount
15. Balloon Date – If there is a balloon payment on the note
16. Remarks - Account active, closed by credit grantor, closed by consumer, consumer disputes, etc.
17. Public Records – judgments, foreclosures, bankruptcy, etc.
18. Inquiries – new credit inquiries or updates from existing creditors.

How to Improve Your Credit Scores?

Credit scoring is done by computer. The computer gives points for positive information and takes away points for negative information. It is important to understand how credit scores are calculated so you can beat the system and manipulate your score.

1. 35 percent of the score is based on your payment history.

All your credit cards, installment accounts, car loans, mortgage loans are listed on your credit report and stays there. The longer the history, the better is your score. Therefore, if you want to cancel any credit card, cancel the newer ones and keep the oldest ones which will help your credit score. On the other hand, the shorter your credit history, the greater the effect delinquent payments could have on your score. A perfect history will show no late payments. Your score will be deducted if there are late payments shown. Whether you miss payment on an $80 cable TV bill or missing a $2,500 mortgage payment, it could adversely affect your rating by as much as 100 points. Score deductions started to escalate if there are multiple delinquents and/or longer delinquent days. If you ever have a late bill go into collections, it becomes a major negative impact on your credit rating. However, as the adverse items become older, the deduction becomes less. More recent delinquents are red flags to creditors that you may still be in financial trouble. In comparison, if you missed a couple of payments many years ago but not since will not affect your score as much.

Late payment items will be removed from your credit history after seven years. To avoid late payments, you should always pay at least one week prior to the due date to allow time for mail or on line payment to go through. If your payment arrived one day late, not only that you will be paying a late fee, the thirty to fifty-nine day late will stay on your credit record for seven years.

2. 30 percent of the score is based on Revolving Debt Ratio.

This is based on the total amount of credit cards you owe, divided by your total available credit line. For example, if you have two credit cards with $10,000 limit each, and you owe a total of $2,500, your ratio is 25 percent. The best credit scores are derived from a debt ratio below 30 percent usage but, as much as possible, try to stay below 50 percent or your score will start dropping significantly. This is an area you can manipulate your score the most. Keep more credit cards or credit limits even if you do not need them. Do not cancel the cards you do not use. This will keep your total available credit high so whatever you owe will end up with a mush lower ratio, thus higher credit score. Also, on the cards you do not normally use, use them occasionally. Otherwise, your credit card issuer may close your inactive cards without notice. Even if you have the money to pay, you should leave some balance occasionally. The system wants to see that you are still using the credit and using it "responsibly", like monthly installment payments. If you do not use the credit, it gives no input to the computer rating system. The best practice is to keep all your credit cards open and rotate them so you are only using one or two every month. As long as you do not have high balances or missed payments on any of the cards, you will score high on this system. You may also want to call your existing credit cards to increase your limit just to reduce your ratio. Most credit card companies will allow you to increase your limit once every six months, provided your credit met their approval. In the current financial crisis, the Federal Reserve reported that lenders have reduced 65 percent of existing customers' credit card limits. Such actions without notice will result in lower credit scores because lower credit limits will bring higher debt ratio.

3. 15 percent of your score is based of the age of debts.

This is quite simple, the older the credit, the better. So keep the older accounts open. Do not keep getting new accounts and close old ones. Newly applied credits will also hurt your score under "inquiries". Do not open a bunch of new accounts all at once. Such action will hurt your credit score because it reflects to the lenders you are desperate to raise a lot of money in a hurry.

4. 10 percent of the score is based on a mix of credit.

The best combination is one mortgage loan, one auto loan and two to five credit cards. Diversity helps your credit score. Mortgage loans and auto installment loans can tell your creditor how responsible you are in making monthly payments one time over along duration. This is where some rich people may score low because they pay cash to buy homes or cars. Therefore, even if you have the money, try finance a small portion of your house or car just to establish your payment history and a mixture of loans to manipulate your score.

5. Last 10 percent of your score is based on Inquiries within the past two years.

Inquiries of your credit report from existing creditors, insurance companies, utility companies, and yourself will not affect your credit score. Only inquiries for new credit will cause your score to drop slightly. If you are shopping for a home loan from five different lenders around the same time, it will be considered as one single inquiry because the system will recognize you were simply shopping around for the same loan. However, if you have excessive inquiries from applying new credit cards all at one time, that could bring your credit score down significantly because it appears you are desperate for money. Therefore, make sure you do not go around and apply new credit cards all at once blindly. Spread them out and add new credit cards once every six months.

Aside from the components that add up to your final credit score, any public record showing bankruptcies, judgments, tax liens, or foreclosures will seriously damage your score. There is a huge deduction of score when any of these serious events shown on your report. However, as these adverse items get older, the impact is lessened. A chapter 13 filed six years ago has very little score deduction as compared to one filed recently. While chapter 13 and foreclosure will stay on your credit report for seven years, a chapter 7 liquidation bankruptcy will stay there for ten years. A judgment will stay on your report until it is satisfied, dismissed or released by court. As I pointed out earlier, if a foreclosure shown on your credit report, you will have to wait at least four years before you can qualify for a Fannie Mae mortgage loan.

The scoring system does not factor in the assets you own. It does not matter if you own a lot of assets or have a significant net worth. The only things counted are those listed above. This is why the system has its flaws and the score can be manipulated. Although each credit bureau applies similar system to derive your credit score, they are not the same. In fact, sometimes their scores could vary greatly. This is because they use different scales on the evaluation and not every one picks up the same information (e.g. a creditor made an inquiry from one credit bureau so the other two will not pick up such inquiry). It is not uncommon sometimes one or more of them simply missing some information. This is why you should order and review all three reports from time to time to make sure there are no mistakes.

Regardless of all the above things to help you manipulate your credit score, there is nothing better than simply pay at least the minimum payments on time each month.

Credit Traps

As the recession lingers, more and more people live on paycheck to paycheck. Sometimes, they are desperate in need of some quick cash to pay bills before the next paycheck arrives. They may resort to pawn shops or payday loans for relief. These operations are essentially loan sharks. You may be writing a check for $250 to get $200 cash. The payday loan company then cashes your check in about two weeks. You may not be aware but you could be paying 400 percent to 600 percent annual rate of interest! These payday loan shops are popping up all over the place.

About the Author

Andrew C. Mungar has been a well-respected real estate expert in Texas for thirty years. He is one of the top real estate developers in Texas, having developed award- winning, large planned communities in excess of 1,000 acres. Thousands of families have lived in homes built by or in communities developed by Mr. Mungar, including many world-renowned celebrities.

Mr. Mungar has been a licensed a real estate broker, and a member of the National Association of Realtors, for over twenty-five years. He owns a realty firm to serve homeowners, investors, lenders, tenants, and landlords, both residential and commercial. He also provides consulting services to investors, builders, developers, lenders, and government agencies. His extensive experience and knowledge covers real estate development, construction, homebuilding, mortgages, finance, management, sales, and marketing.

The Greater Houston Builders Association honored Mr. Mungar with the prestigious Harris B. Lieberman Distinguished Service Award, given each year to one person for outstanding service and dedication to

Houston's construction industry and its trade association. Mr. Mungar also received many other top awards such as Entrepreneur of the Year and Developer of the Year.

The State of Texas appointed Mr. Mungar to serve on a Toll Road Authority. The City of Houston appointed Mr. Mungar to serve on the board of a Redevelopment Authority and a Tax Increment Reinvestment Zone. City of Missouri City appointed Mr. Mungar to serve on numerous committees. In addition, Mr. Mungar served on the Fort Bend County Economic Development Board and the Chamber of Commerce. In 2005, Mr. Mungar was an expert witness and testified on behalf of the IRS and U.S. Attorney's Office against several mortgage fraud scam artists.

Mr. Mungar has a degree in accounting and finance. He was one of just a few developers who survived Houston's deepest recession in the mid-eighties and gained great experience in how to survive through a major housing bubble. Mr. Mungar now devotes his time to helping and teaching homeowners needing assistance. He is teaching homeowner seminars across the State of Texas. This book contains not only his personal experiences but lots of valuable insider information through anonymous interviews and research of other consultants, loss mitigation negotiators, homeowners, fund managers, attorneys, and government officials. This is one of the most comprehensive guidebooks ever written; all homeowners should have this book in case of emergency.

LaVergne, TN USA
27 August 2009
156136LV00004B/5/P